American Beauties: Rose and Tulip Quilts

by
Gwen Marston & Joe Cunningham

American Quilter's Society

P.O. Box 3290 • Paducah, Kentucky 42001

Credits

All photographs by The KEVA Partnership, Flint, Michigan, unless otherwise noted.
All drawings by Gwen Marston and Russell Scheffer.

Additional copies of this book may be ordered from:

American Quilter's Society
P.O. Box 3290
Paducah, KY 42001

@$14.95. Add $2.00 for postage and handling.

Contents

Preface 4

Introduction 5

American Beauties 8

Gallery of Quilts 20

How We Work 42

Patterns 45

Appendix 88

References 90

Index of Quilts, Blocks and Patterns 92

Bibliography 93

Preface

This book suggested itself to us several years ago when we first realized that our applique quilts were . . . strange. Why, we wondered, were mid-19th century **pieced** quilts seen as extraordinary artistic achievements, often replicated and studied by contemporary quiltmakers, while applique quilts from the same period were virtually ignored?

In trying to understand how these quilts were made and what happened to them during this revival, we talked to quilters across the country, studied quilts and books and made quilts.

One of our chief resources in this, as in many of our projects, was Mary Schafer, a great quiltmaker and collector from Michigan. She has been our mentor, friend and advisor for over 10 years. As curators of her collection, we have been able to study many fine quilts in detail and at length. Many of our favorites from her collection are included here.

One of Mary's unusual endeavors has been to complete a number of quilts which her friend Betty Harriman started. Betty was a great quiltmaker from Missouri who made her first quilt the year Mary was born, 1910. She continued to make quilts throughout her life. She and Mary became friends through the mail in the 1960's. When Betty died in 1971, Mary acquired all her unfinished work and set about finishing it. A complete account of the relationship between these two women and their quilts is available in the 1986 volume of "Uncoverings," the research papers of the American Quilt Study Group. (Available from the AQSG, 105 Molino Ave., Mill Valley, CA 94941.) We mention it here because a number of the quilts in this book were the results of this unusual "collaboration."

Mary has made many floral appliques, including rose and tulip designs. Most of ours have been tulips. In our discussions of old fashioned applique, we decided we could illustrate most of our ideas and theories by limiting the book to roses and tulips, the most popular subjects of old applique designs.

All our quilts, Mary's and our own, are hand appliqued and hand quilted of cotton fabric unless noted otherwise in the captions. The only difference in our techniques is that we do most of our piecing on the machine, while Mary does everything by hand.

This book has a discussion of our ideas, a description of how applique evolved in American quiltmaking, photographs of quilts from our collections and some of our favorite patterns. Following the main part of the book is a reference section which lists examples of rose and tulip quilts published in other books you may have.

This book would not have been possible – we might not even be so involved with quilts – without the continued help and inspiration we receive from Mary Schafer, who shared her collection of quilts, documents and materials with us, answered numberless questions and made blocks for this project. Preparing the manuscript we also turned repeatedly to the knowledgable, tireless Cuesta Benberry, who generously answered questions, shared source materials, loaned blocks from her collection and agreed to let us reprint her article on state rose patterns in the appendix. Barbara Brackman has helped not only by publishing so much valuable information on patterns and dates, but also by answering our questions about specific materials and patterns. Hildagard Hoag made the Old English Rose for us to use in this book. Bets Ramsey sent us the up-to-date information on the Tennessee quilt project. We sincerely thank Mary, Cuesta, Barbara, Bets and Hilda for their help.

We also thank quilters who voluntarily sent us patterns, photographs of family quilts and information about rose and tulip quilts which was helpful in the preparation of this book: Kay Spangler, Laura Rodin, Margaret Moody, Linda Hoemke, Rosie Grimstead, Bonnie Hobbs, Barbara Dimock, Gerry Rohwer, Lois Donaldson, Joyce Whittier, Jane Braverman, Marge Ragle, Dorothy Houseman, Aileen Smith, Barbara Lower and Muriel Douglas.

Introduction

By the time we two began making quilts together in 1979, serious quiltmakers and quilt artists virtually all agreed that the pieced quilt was the one with the most potential for abstract graphic design, the stated and unstated aim of much of the art quilt movement. We, too, began our "serious" work with pieced quilts in the most abstract traditional style: Amish. We did not want anyone to think we were making fluffy, poofey, dandified decorator's items. We wanted to convey our own familiarity with the "rules" of modern, hard-edged abstraction.

It was not long before we had to re-evaluate our stance. Too many of our favorite old quilts were appliqued. Soon we started to wonder about our own notion of "toughness" and abstraction; were we imposing arbitrary standards on quilts? Tough abstraction is a concept defined by 20th century, mostly male painters – what did it have to do with 19th century, mostly female quiltmakers? What was wrong with delicate realism? And who said applique quilts could not be tough, anyway?

We studied these questions the same way we study any quilt-related issue, by making quilts. We copied simple, bold appliques, intricate, delicate appliques, appliqued borders and blocks. Before long we saw that there was no such thing as "the" applique quilt. Appliqued quilts were as varied as pieced. Some were boldly original, some were timidly ordinary. Many were somewhere in between, using common ideas in original ways. If we wanted strong graphic design, we could find it; if we wanted elegant, symmetrical patterns, they were abundant.

We found that we preferred the splashy, red and green four-block applique quilts. Their appeal is in their large-scale boldness – not in the awesome virtuosity of their technique. But in talking to quilters around the country, we realized that the contemporary approach to applique had more in common with the Baltimore Bride's type of work than with the kind we liked best. Some quilters, we found, felt intimidated by applique. Thinking that it took too long, that they were not up to its technical demands, or thinking that making applique quilts would automatically separate them from the art world, many quilters simply rejected the technique.

Eventually, we began to reach new conclusions. The chief reason for the predominance of piecing in this quilting revival, we think, is fashion, just as fashion has been responsible for nearly all developments in quiltmaking. Today, abstract pieced quilts are giving way to the more newly fashionable ambiguous, figurative, post-modern art quilts, many of which are machine or hand appliqued. Still, among quilt artists, floral appliques are little made because they do not fit into the current aesthetic. In other words – floral appliques are not artistically fashionable.

That has not stopped many contemporary quilters from making floral appliques, however. There is a strong contingent of quilters who have always been indifferent to what is currently popular. Over the years we have seen many fine contemporary appliqued quilts, and we have studied them as assiduously as we have studied the old ones. One of our favorite contemporary quilters is Mary Johnson, from Munster, Indiana. A great example of her work is her BIRD OF PARADISE shown in the *Quilt Art Engagement Calendar 1988*. (Also shown on page 31 in the Fall, 1987 issue of *American Quilter*.) Based on a famous quilt owned by The Museum of American Folk Art, Mary's BIRD OF PARADISE is a virtuoso effort, made not for the art gallery, or the quilt judge, but herself. We are sure Mary **understands** the original in ways no one can without making the quilt. Incidentally, another of our favorite contemporary quiltmakers, Laverne Mathews of Orange, Texas, has an applique quilt on page 30 of the same *American Quilter*. Laverne has been making quilts since 1971 and makes them **her** way, devising her own patterns and working freely.

In 1983 or so, we noticed something about our own applique quilts: all our floral applique quilts contained tulip designs. In an effort to finish our "tulip phase" once and for all, we decided to make a tulip sampler, with which we could make all the different blocks we wanted on a single quilt. It did not work. Almost as soon as we took the sampler out of the frame we were at work on another tulip pattern.

Mary Schafer, our mentor and quilt "counselor," did not share our obsession with tulip designs. She preferred roses. We all shared the same preferrence, however, for the bolder, unusual appliques.

Accordingly, our techniques are very simple by today's standards. While there are many new approaches to making ever more precise and exacting patterns, we have continued to use the most basic techniques and tools for sewing one piece of cloth onto another. We have stayed with our methods during this revolutionary period because our goals have little to do with that which new techniques are intended to affect.

Changes in applique technique have affected it drastically, and these changes reflect the current attitudes toward what applique should be. The aim of nearly any new technique is to remove the element of chance from the quiltmaking process. This is a natural result of the quest for artistic legitimacy. Artists, it is thought, need to be in control of every aspect of their creation. Also, whether or not a quilt is to be entered in a contest, most are made according to contest rules.

Appliqued vines, therefore, should not be allowed to wander along any meandering path they choose, starting and stopping at corners, asymmetrically and lazily waving to one another across the quilt. They should have the same number of the same curves on each side, and all four corners should be the same.

Special paper, glue and drafting tools are required to make each block an exact replication of the pattern, as if each block were made by a flawless machine. All stitches must be chastely hidden, not nakedly flaunted.

This is all new. Most mid-19th century appliques were made **within a format**, not **with a pattern**. Certainly, some quiltmakers had more exacting techniques, more of a disposition for organization than others and so made more symmetrical quilts. But many of the finest of those appliques show plenty of evidence that chance and individuality played large roles in their design. Many shapes were obviously cut freehand from the cloth. Leaves, stems, buds and flowers often appear in different positions on each block. Many of the floral appliques were made of scraps instead of all new yardage.

As interesting, even beautiful, antiques, these quilts may appeal strongly to us. Yet, by the prevailing standards of today, these powerful works are not symmetrical enough to win prizes, not complicated enough to be technically awesome, not artistic enough in the modern sense to warrant emulation. It is hardly surprising that the common appliqued designs of the 19th century have not been revived or explored as seriously as the common pieced designs have been.

We made our wreath quilt (Plate 12) as an imitation of those common, unorganized scrap appliques which were made with no pattern, only an idea. The idea was to make a wreath with flowers, leaves and stems, then to surround it with an applique border made in panels – four wavy vines that did not match and did not meet at the corners. To keep the flavor of the quilts we were imitating, we cut all the shapes freehand from scraps. We made no sketches before we started and made no templates as we worked along.

The finished quilt exemplifies a quilt judge's nightmare. Nothing matches; nothing is coordinated. One of the sawtooth borders did not work out evenly in the corner. None of its irregularities would bar it from an art gallery, but there it would fail as being unoriginal – which it is – and because of its unarty color scheme. All in all, it is an example of the kind of quilt that had become nearly defunct as 20th century quiltmaking evolved first toward quilts made from patterns, then toward quilts made as art. There is little place for it outside our home.

This, we feel, is the central issue in the evolution of modern quiltmaking: quilts have become public. Like television programs, quilts today must compete for market shares. Old quilts must appeal to collectors if they are to be considered worthwhile. New quilts must meet the requirements of the art world, or the standards of a quilt judge. At the least, many quiltmakers feel the need to justify their work to the members of their guild. Many would be embarrassed to show our wreath quilt at the monthly Show & Tell.

We are not embarrassed to include it in our book because it succeeds in the way we intended. This is the quilt we set out to make. Most important, we did not make it for anyone else, only ourselves – the same audience for whom we make all our quilts.

It is **because** quilts are "public" that we have access to the thousands of great quilts that have inspired us. And it is because quilts are public that we are able to consider quiltmaking as a profession. But it is also this publicness that inculcates anxiety and pressure to conform among many quiltmakers. Oddly, one of the strongest of these pressures is to be "original."

We can say our Rose and Tulip wreath is all original. We made it up. But that is not exactly what most people have in mind when they say or think, "Be Original." What they have in mind is to be original in ways that fit with current concepts of art and quiltmaking. The net effect of this line of thought is that, while this type of quilt might appeal to many people if it were 100-years-old, it is also the kind of quilt that few of us make today – because we "know better." We know better than to start with no plan. We know better than to use a boring old color scheme. We know better than to make the vine borders one at a time or to use scraps all of the same print density.

In fact, floral appliques largely fall into the category of quilts that serious quiltmakers think are too cute and artless. Those who do choose to make floral appliques most often attempt to reproduce one type only – the perfectly symmetrical, regular, coordinated type. Great quilts can be made this way, as the quilts by Mary Schafer, Betty Harriman and others in this book show. Still, we think it is strange that new pieced quilts are often modeled on the simplest, most primitive antique quilts, while new applique quilts almost never are.

This makes sense if we accept the truism that "quilts are art." If quilts are indeed art, then quiltmakers must be artists. If quiltmakers are artists, then they must follow the paths all modern artists must follow, including the path which leads to public acceptance. No artist in her right mind then would waste her time making a series of highly artless red and green floral appliques.

If it was common for 19th century quiltmakers to make both pieced and appliqued quilts, and if many of those appliques were red and green floral appliques, then why should we ignore them? If we are going to say that we are carrying on a long tradition, why should we study only those parts of the tradition that resemble something else? We think it is difficult enough to make sense of quilts without imposing the concepts of another discipline upon them.

We have tried to educate ourselves about quilts not to become artists, but rather, "quiltists." In that way, we consider all the work we have done so far our "student work." We have been and continue to be students of quilts, working toward a level of understanding and ability which we hope will allow us to contribute meaningfully to their development.

It was as quiltists that we began making applique quilts. At first, we decided to explore applique because we felt it was our duty – important, we felt, for our quilt education. Neither of us was passionate about floral applique. Gwen had an applique quilt started when she met Joe, a tulip from *The Standard Book of Quiltmaking*, by Margaret Ickis (Plate 37). Not knowing what she did or did not like about applique, she chose a pattern almost at random, deciding that the important thing was to start. Joe's first applique was on a WILD GOOSE CHASE quilt shown in our book *Sets and Borders* (AQS, 1987). Having learned the basics of applique technique, we ventured from pattern to pattern, copying the Giant Tulip, making the Smithsonian Tulip and others from patterns.

After we made our sampler in 1984, we abandoned patterns altogether and started to work in the styles of various old quilts we liked. Only when we examined our quilts for this book did we realize that we had developed definite tastes: our later quilts are larger in scale, often four-block sets, freer and more expressive than our early ones.

In other words, we saw that we had worked backward through the history of American applique. We had started with the modern style of working from a pattern, very precise and controlled, and eventually found ourselves making the earliest types of applique – working within formats rather than with patterns, very loose and imprecise. Along the way we also made plume quilts, folded paper design quilts, even an eagle quilt, in our effort to learn more about 19th century applique.

Our student work, then, is not drudgery. We love making quilts. Our search through their history has been full of discovery and wonder. It was amazing to discover about appliqued rose and tulip designs that, more important than the design we chose, was the attitude with which we worked. While it may be possible to reproduce some of the great old quilts by imitating their "flaws" and irregularities, the only way we have discovered to make quilts like those we admired is to adopt the attitude which we think produced them in the first place.

That attitude of acceptance toward our quilts, accepting that the quilts will reveal themselves as we work, is directly opposed to the more common attitude today: that a quiltmaker must plan each detail first, usually by making a scale drawing on graph paper, then impose her will upon the quilt in progress to make sure it nowhere gets out of hand. We try to trust the process of quiltmaking to determine what our quilts will look like.

We have tried to foster the attitude of "trusting the process" in all our quiltmaking, not only in the details of our quilts, but also in our lives as quiltmakers. We think that the only way we will be able to reach our goal of making great quilts is to go through the same process great quiltmakers of the past went through: learn the techniques, copy the quilts we like, and make quilts as if it were an enjoyable part of everyday life.

There are ironies in all this. It seems that the less we worry about being original the more original our quilts look. Our latest, loosest quilts were made with the surest hands. The less we try to express ourselves the more expressive out quilts become. The less we seek results the more we enjoy the process – and the stronger the results.

In *The Crafts Report* of October, 1987, we saw an article which explained better than we could how we approached quilts. It was an article about a group of Japanese craftspersons visiting the United States to see American crafts. One mentioned the late folk-style potter Shoji Hamada, who "took pains to avoid producing work that 'smelled' of himself." The author paraphrased the craftsman by saying that, ". . . striving to impose one's personality on one's work tends to destroy the beauty in it that is beyond the individual human being."

In the article the craftsmen talked about another idea foreign to much American craft: Shinichi Shioyasu, a maker of Wajima laquerware, when asked to comment on work in a show here, said, "Simplify . . . Think of what the material is trying to say instead of what you want it to say."

That is what we have tried to do with our quilts in this book. As **quiltists** we have tried to let our quilts be quilts, instead of trying to make them be art. Making quilts we will inevitably express ourselves, but we want first to let the quilts say what they will.

These rose and tulip appliques represent one side of the work of some unknown quiltmakers from the past, as well as some early and late 20th century quiltmakers. We present our quilts with the others, fully realizing how insignificant they must appear by comparison.

1. Martha Washington Rose, by Mary Schafer, 1971, 10″. Collection of Cuesta Benberry.

The pink center pieces are closely abutted, barely allowing the red underneath to show through. Mary's pattern lists this as Progressive Farmer *pattern #1928. (See pattern #3.)*

American

Applique has changed, and its changes have not been simple swings of fashion – although fashion has always played its role, making one pattern or technique popular this year, another one the next – but fundamental, drastic changes in every aspect of applique quiltmaking, from drafting the pattern to quilting the finished top. To see how rose and tulip quilts in particular have been affected by these changes, we have to look at applique in general. We need to talk about how applique began here as a handy technique that lead to one of the first fads in quiltmaking; how it soon developed into a new branch on the needlework family tree and flowered in the middle of the last century; how it eventually came to be seen as a difficult, fussy technique to be used mostly for virtuoso, elaborate patterns, cut off from the most artistic branches of contemporary quiltmaking. While there are a few pieced blocks in this book, we are chiefly concerned with applique.

Applique was not invented in the United States. Perhaps because of its use for repairs, the technique has been around as long as cloth. The oldest quilted object of which we are aware – a quilted carpet from first century B.C. Mongolia – has appliqued fighting beasts, appliqued spiral designs, even an appliqued border. And, from earliest times, flowers have provided all types of needleworkers with thematic material, so neither was floral applique invented here.

The first widespread use of floral applique in the New World was in the "Broderie Perse" type of quilts. These were the beautiful and now famous quilts made by cutting flowers, trees, birds, insects or other designs from handsome, printed chintzes and appliqueing them onto a new background cloth, usually white cotton or linen. Most Broderie Perse quilts used the medallion format, with a central design – such as a tree of life, a vase of flowers, or a bird of paradise – surrounded by one or more "frames," or borders. These quilts date mostly from 1750 to 1825, and they naturally enough resemble the Indian cotton "Palampores" in fashion in Europe at the time. Broderie Perse quilts seem to have been very popular in the colonies, and some of the first textiles to be printed there were printed with special urns, flowers, butterflies and other designs custom made for the technique.

American invention, however, soon developed new kinds of applique designs which did not require expensive chintz or serpentine edges to be cut and sewn. The

2. Mexican Rose, by the authors, 1987, 18″. Collection of the authors.

The diamond-shaped leaves indicate that this pattern came from a very old block. Few diamond-shaped leaves appear on quilts after the mid-19th century. According to Hall and Kretsinger this pattern is from "c. 1842." (See pattern #4.)

Beauties

new block designs could be made of common calicoes or even home-dyed, homespun fabric. In place of the extremely realistic chintz flowers came the more simplified, abstract floral designs, like Whig Rose and Rose of Sharon. Block-style quilts gained such prominence that by shortly after 1800, they were perhaps more popular than medallions. Most of the designers of these new patterns made no attempt to portray a flower realistically, choosing instead to signify certain flowers with shapes from a growing vocabulary of leaves, petals and stems.

These designers were not professional designers like we have today, they were the quiltmakers themselves, who, instead of regarding patterns as fixed sets of template shapes requiring exact duplication, regarded patterns as formats for quilt designs. They fashioned their quilts much as a poet fashions a sonnet – the form may be the same as others, but no two are alike. With the emphasis today on **patterns**, these old quilts can be difficult to understand.

The appliqued vine borders of mid-19th century quilts, for instance, often seem ineptly designed: they just start and stop will-nilly, curving here and there without symmetry or corner resolution. Leaves and flowers sometimes seem to have been cut without the benefit of templates, and placed without the aid of a pattern. Even the blocks of some old quilts do not match, with some leaves turned this way, some that, each blossom seeming to be another variation on the theme of the supposed pattern. Further, many of these quilts are made of red and green fabric on a white background – Christmas colors. And, to some, it seems a shame the quiltmakers were not more consistent with names and patterns.

If you were making quilts in the early 19th century and you wanted to make a Whig Rose pattern, you might decide to use three or four concentric, wavy rings for the middle. Then you might or might not add the four, more or less hand-shaped, projections from the center. You would probably include four stems – narrow or wide, curved or straight – with leaves and buds projecting outward from the central bloom. With the optional doo-dads around the middle, and all the possible interpretations of the shapes, your quilt would be unique, as nearly all Whig Roses were. Thus, the reason it is so difficult to find two

3. Michigan Rose, by Mary Schafer, 1987, 12″. Collection of the authors.

Mary designed this block in honor of the Michigan Sesquecentennial. (See pattern #5.)

4. Old English Rose, by Hildagard Hoag, 1987, 24″. Collection of the authors.

Of the many patterns which include both roses and tulips, we think this is one of the loveliest. Our friend Hilda generously agreed to make it for this book.

The pattern was brought to America from England in 1839. Almost a century later Charlotte Jane Whitehill combined it with a Kentucky Rose pattern in one of her stunning quilts, shown in The Romance of the Patchwork Quilt in America. *(See pattern #7.)*

5. Rose, maker unknown, c. 1840-65, 22½″. Collection of the authors.

This block is a classic example of mid-19th century applique. The original design is beautifully thought out and executed. The applique was done with white thread and a tiny whip stitch. The yellow center was reverse appliqued.

Everything about this block, including the information we received from the dealer, leads us to think it was made in Pennsylvania.

matching Whig Roses today is that Whig Rose was a format, not a pattern.

The same held true of other ideas for rose patterns. Among rose appliques there were few types, but numberless variations. To further confuse the matter, 20th century writers have often ascribed names to quilt patterns, based on educated guesses. What some call "Whig Rose," others call "Rose of Sharon." We find it most helpful to disregard the pattern names, new or old, when we study old quilts in preparing to make a new one. Instead, we examine quilts of the design type or format in which we are interested. In the 19th century, there were only 6 or 7 primary formats for rose patterns, each made of a similar vocabulary of shapes:

1. The Whig Rose format, with its complex center and four curved branches. (See any of the WHIG ROSES in this book, as well as DEMOCRATIC ROSE, Plate 3.)
2. The Center Rose, a simple, slightly abstracted rose flower seen from above, with leaf points or buds, but no stem. (See LEE'S ROSE AND BUDS, Plate 5.)
3. The Central Stem, a realistic picture of a rose on a stem, often with branches, leaves, buds or secondary blossoms. (See ROSE OF SHARON, Plate 13.)
4. The Rose Wreath, a fairly large ring, usually supporting four roses and a number of leaves. (See ROSE WREATH, Plate 16.)
5. The Crossed Rose, roses on the ends of crossed stems, sometimes with a fancy center or leaves. (See MEXICAN ROSE. Block 2.)
6. The Rose Tree, a large "U" shape with fancy roses, many leaves and buds. (See MISSOURI ROSE TREE, Plate 7.)
7. The Flower Pot, some type of pot or basket containing any number of roses. (Similar to TULIP POT, Plate 39.)

Some of these formats were common to applique pattern based on other flowers, such as tulips. From the information we have gathered, we think tulip patterns were the second most popular in the last century. Like rose formats, there were Crossed Tulip, (See CROSSED TULIP, Plate 23, or HOLLAND QUEEN, Plate 27.) Tulip Wreath, (See block in PENN. DUTCH FLOWER GARDEN, Plate 30.) Tulip Flower Pot, (See TULIP POT, Plate 39.) and Large Tulip on a Stem (See GIANT TULIP, Plate 25.) formats. One other format, called "Single Tulip," is made of three appliqued tulips on stems. (See SINGLE TULIP, Plate 32.)

Some 19th century patterns, both rose and tulip, were based partly or completely on pieced flowers. There are two main types of these pieced patterns, one with flowers made of diamonds and one circular type.

1. PIECED Tulip, sometimes called "Peony," or "Li-

6. Rose and Tulip, maker unknown, c. 1875-1900, 36″. Collection of the authors.

We know nothing about this block, except for the possibility that it came from Ohio, where the dealer acquired it. Its solid-color fabric gives little clue to its date.

ly,'' based on an early star pattern. According to Ruth Finley in OLD PATCHWORK QUILTS:

"In patchwork the diamond produced a number of patterns exclusively the quilt's own that were at once floral and geometrical. These are based on the famous 'LeMoyne Star' and include all the pieced 'lily' and 'tulip' designs.'' (P. 89)

(See CLEVELAND TULIP, Plate 22.)

2. FULL-BLOWN TULIP, a difficult, circular design with eight points, small half-circles and four curved inset pieces in the center. (See FULL-BLOWN TULIP, Plate 24.)

This type of design is so abstract that it could be said to represent nearly anything one wants. Accordingly, it has many names, many variations. The rose version is called "Harrison Rose," and it has a stem.

During the heyday of the red and green applique quilt – from about 1825 to 1875 – thousands of similar quilts were made and, studying the surviving ones today, we can see that each quiltmaker had her own idea about what constituted a particular pattern. While we have tried to classify quilts into these broad categories, there are large numbers of quilts which do not fit into the confines of even the most flexible definition, being unique creations by independent quiltmakers.

Fewer floral appliques were made in the last quarter of the century, and by 1900, quilting was practiced mostly in rural communities, about the time the population of the United States became predominantly urban – leaving the rural, quiltmaking segment in the minority. This set the stage for the first nostalgic quilt revival of this century, and a new kind of applique became popular almost overnight. When patterns began to be published in large numbers, appliqued as well as pieced patterns lost some of their vitality. With fewer people creating the patterns, they lost much of their diversity.

Between 1910 and 1920, quilts became marketable. Magazine columns were devoted to quilts and quilt patterns. Pattern companies sprang up to meet the demand. Crazy quilts, which had been fashionable in the last quarter of the 19th century, were supplanted by newly revived or created pieced and appliqued patterns. The new applique patterns had definite names and pattern pieces. The old red and green color scheme was out; new pastels were in.

One of the best quilt designers of the period was Marie Webster of Marion, Indiana. In her 1915 book, *Quilts: Their Story and How to Make Them*, she showed not only many fine antique quilts, but also a number of new quilts of her own design. Obviously influenced by the then contemporary "Arts and Crafts" movement, her designs made a near complete break with those of the previous century. She designed rose and tulip patterns, as well as

7. Rose Wreath, by Mary Schafer, 1987, 13″. Collection of the authors.

Mary made this block as an example of the archetypical rose wreath. (See pattern #9.)

8. Rosebud, by the authors, 1985, 12″. Collection of the authors.

One of more than 40 pieced rose patterns we have seen, most from this century, Rosebud was published by the Ladies Art Company in 1928 and later by Progressive Farmer *as pattern #1640. (See pattern #10.)*

9. San Jose Rose, by Mary Schafer, 1980, 12½". Collection of the authors.

This block was a Christmas gift to Cuesta from Mary. It is one of the many rose patterns named for states or cities.

dozens of others, and sold them all through the mail. Although we have no examples of her tulip or rose patterns, the patterns shown on page 19 demonstrate her approach quite clearly: pastel colors, artful and symmetrical design, defiantly "modern" and unlike their 19th century forebears.

As they had not learned quiltmaking when they were young, more and more women relied on magazine columns and published patterns like Marie's for their information on quilts. In order to teach quiltmaking, authors had to classify, organize and reduce that process which had formerly been almost anarchic. Quilting neophytes received patterns passively instead of creating them themselves; they learned the techniques from published step-by-step instructions instead of absorbing them naturally from an early age; they viewed quilts as something from the past which they could learn to **recreate**, instead of creating naturally in the first place.

Aside from encouraging women to take up quiltmaking, published patterns led inevitably to pattern collecting, so there appeared at least two new classes of people interested in quilts: quilt writer/designers and pattern collectors. This meant there was a resurgence of interest in quilts, but it did not necessarily mean more quilts of a wider variety would be made. Significantly, during the period when thousands of patterns were first published and collected – 1900 to 1940 – relatively few patterns actually made the transition from paper to cloth. Nearly all patterns took on a new symmetry and refinement. For, in order to prepare a pattern for printing, authors had to straighten, smooth, simplify, redraw and clean up the often rough, asymmetrical lines of the original – just as we have had to do here. New quilters came to see these refined patterns as "correct," and the original quilts from which they were taken as "incorrect," a concept which is still with us.

With a few notable exceptions – Webster, Finley, Hall and Kretsinger – the literature of quilting during the 30's and 40's came to be dominated by the "cute home furnishings" and "easy project for beginners" type of writing. Instructions for quilted bath mats, tea towels, tea cozies, pillows and other simple projects were aimed at the modern woman, who was presumably too busy to make a quilt.

Vera C. Alexander, author of *Patchwork and Applique*, (1930) gives instructions for "Shadow Applique," "Bulk Applique," "Loose Applique," "Net Applique," and several others, together with a book full of ideas for implementing the techniques in making chair, telephone and seat covers, bags, coats, shawls, pictures and, at last, a "Cretonne Applique" quilt! She qualifies her comments

10. Wild Rose, by Mary Schafer, 1971, 12". Collection of Cuesta Benberry.

Mary received this pattern in one of the "round robin" pattern exchanges in which she participated during the 1960's.

This rose is one of the simplest of all, perhaps one of the oldest as well. We publish the pattern in Lady's Circle Patchwork Quilts, *January, 1988, in our column on applique for beginners.*

carefully when it comes to the full-size quilt:

"Bedspreads! That leads one to think of quilts, and quilts suggest patchwork! Before starting on the subject of patchwork quilts, I would like to add that cretonne applique can be used on any article, no matter what size, providing the applique is in proportion." (P. 92)

The changes in attitudes during the first part of this century were only the beginning. With the resurgence of interest in quilts in the late 1960's and 1970's came even more fundamental shifts in how quilts were perceived.

Quiltmaking only had to be relearned in the early decades of this century; it had to be virtually excavated and restored in the later decades. Contemporary quiltmakers who learned from someone in their family are extremely rare. Most of us have taken lessons from teachers or books. The result is that modern quiltmaking is a new creation with new concepts of beauty, new goals, new customs. This is as it should be. But we feel that even though old applique quilts have been much studied as important historical and social documents, they have been little studied as the basis of the new quiltmaking. Only the quilts that happened to fit in with 20th century artistic tastes have been emulated and studied. The parts of the tradition that fell outside those tastes have not inspired the same enthusiasm.

Quilt design of the last century was made up of three equal parts: piecework, applique and quilting design. Because of their resemblance to modern painting and for other reasons, pieced quilts drew the attention of intellectuals of the 1970's. The fact that 19th century quiltmakers anticipated modern artistic discoveries by over 100 years led to intense "chicken-or-the-egg" debates, endless discussions over whether or not these quilts should be seen as art when no one knows the original quiltmaker's intentions, and if quilters had discovered some of the same principles as modern artists, why should the artists get credit for "pioneering?"

The discussions of these topics contributed to the idea that pieced quilts were the most artful and aesthetically successful of all quilt types. Old pieced quilts were collected and praised for their "graphic power." In other words, pieced quilts achieved artistic legitimacy by fitting in with current fashions in art, which in the early 70's were mostly about abstract graphic design. Only recently, since post-modern, neoprimitivism has become fashionable, have we begun to see more quilt artists turn to applique as a technique suitable for the required organic shapes and nervous, post-modern lines. This change can be seen clearly in the Quilt National catalogues, the hand-

11. Dutch Tulip, maker unknown, Tennessee, c. 1930-40, 9″. Collection of the authors.

This is one of a group of 15 blocks collected in Tennessee which had a newspaper clipping attached to them showing an advertisement for the pattern. As the pattern was not with the blocks, we think the quilter probably drafted her own from the ad. Some of the materials are "feed sack" prints.

12. Full Blown Tulip, maker unknown, c. 1865, 12″. Collection of the authors.

This is an old Pennsylvania pattern, which appears in many versions and under a number of titles. It is intricate and difficult to make, which prompted Ruth Finley to say, "Only a soul in desparate need nervous outlet could have conceived and executed, for instance, the Full Blown Tulip." This might have been an original way of piecing the block.

13. Lombardy Lady, by Mary Schafer, 1968, 13″. Collection of Cuesta Benberry.

The four wide tulips are close enough to the leaves to create a "tile work" effect.

some books issued after the artistically prestigious, biannual Quilt National in Athens, Ohio. The early catalogues contain a few, mostly pictorial appliques. The later ones show new applique work which resembles the art of Julian Schnabel, or Keith Haring, to name but two.

Pieced quilts resembled modern art – red and green appliques did not. Of course, masterpiece appliques have long been collected for their value as investments and for the great amount of work they represented. But if you were a quilt collector seeking artistically valuable quilts, or a quilt artist seeking to make the same in the 1970's, pieced quilts were where the action was. Nancy Crow, Michael James, Jeffrey Gutcheon, Nancy Halpern, Jinny Beyers – the most visible quilt artists of the 70's, all made pieced quilts. One of the most influential books of the decade, *The Pieced Quilt* by Jonathon Holstein, clearly and systematically made a case for the artistic superiority of pieced designs over appliqued or quilted designs.

Those less concerned about the intellectual approach have sometimes turned to applique, the second broad segment of quilt design. The modern fashions in applique have been directed less at emulating painting than at emulating the virtuosic Baltimore Bride's quilts, or the influential Rose Kretsinger quilts in the Spencer Museum in Lawrence, Kansas. In place of "graphic power," many modern applique makers have opted for the technically intricate, the minutely controlled, the detailed and awesome types of quilts that signify "technical power." That is why applique has become the technique of choice for making heirloom quilts, as it is thought to be so difficult and time-consuming that the resulting quilt will be seen by succeeding generations as the heroic effort it is.

Quilting designs – the third, formerly equal part quiltmaking – have been little explored during this revival, containing neither graphic force nor instantly overwhelming technical showiness. When quilting designs are taught or discussed, it is nearly always in the context of how they can "support" or "reinforce" the pieced or appliqued design. Almost never is quilting treated as it was on many of the great pieced or appliqued quilts of the past: as if it had a life of its own. On many old quilts the quilting designs have nothing whatsoever to do with the piecing or applique – the quilting lines do not echo, reinforce or otherwise help the piecing or applique, but instead run right over it. In our experience as teachers, we have met many quiltmakers who have taken classes enough to learn more about design and piecing than they could ever use, but who know little or nothing about drafting and marking quilting designs, let alone how to quilt them.

Briefly put, of the many types of quilts made during

14, 15. Tulips, by the authors, 1987, 12″. Collection of the authors.

These two blocks are from the well-known CIRCUIT RIDER'S QUILT in the Chicago Art Institute. It is a sampler made by 40 women for the Rev. G.C. Warvel of the United Bretheren Church of Miami, Ohio, in 1862. The Reverend traveled by horseback on his 6-community circuit and visited each 8 times a year to perform church service, as well as marriages and baptisms. All the blocks are signed. (See patterns #19, #20.)

the last century, some have revived and some have not. Most new quilts are pieced, quite a few are intended as art, very few are in the mold of the vast number of red and green floral appliques of the last century. For a concrete example of how significant a part of the quilt population rose and tulip quilts were in the past, we contacted Bets Ramsey of Quilts of Tennessee, the state documentation project. Almost one-half of the appliqued quilts from before 1930 which the team documented, were either rose or tulip designs. The vast majority of those were primarily red and green.

Of all the red and green floral applique quilts made in the 19th century, rose patterns were the most popular. This is probably because roses have long been the most popular flower in North America. Wild roses grew in every state of the Union, and eventually each state had a rose pattern named for it. (See Cuesta Benberry's article in the Appendix.) Roses appear in songs, in literature and in large bouquets given to mothers on Mothers Day. The passionate reds of roses have often been used to signify romance and love. Perhaps that is why so many Bride's quilts used rose designs.

The ROSE OF SHARON was the last century's favorite among quilters. It was often made by the bride or given as a wedding present – a fitting gift, named for a passage in the Song of Solomon that speaks eloquently of physical as well as spiritual love.

The Whig Rose was popular, too. According to some authors – Ruth Finley, the Orlofsky's – a controversy arose over the quilt pattern between the Whigs and the Democrats, with each party claiming it as its own. DEMOCRATIC ROSE, Plate 3, is simply a WHIG ROSE by another name. It is not surprising that the name was argued. What is surprising is that, given the "free for all" pattern names of the period, more names did not incite arguments.

It is easy to see why rose quilts were made with red and green if you look at a rose. What other colors would you use? Once the fashion for these colors started, it obtained an inertia that perpetuated it. Secondary colors for floral appliques of the period were pink, mustard yellow and orange – more floral colors. Blue and brown were sometimes used, we speculate, as substitutes for green. No doubt they were also used for what they were.

Tulip quilts most often used the same colors, with red and green again being top choice. Tulips were widely cultivated in this country well before 1800, and were especially popular among the Pennsylvania Germans and Dutch. Their folk art is rife with tulips.

We should remember that life in the early-to-mid-1800's was difficult for many women. For all those

See Block 14.

16. Tulip, maker unknown, Philadelphia, c. 1860, 18″. Collection of the authors.

This incomplete block shows how one quilter worked – the patches were basted in place with no guiding marks on the foundation block. As with many tulip patterns, the center section was pieced to the two side parts before the whole tulip was appliqued in place.

17. Tulip, by Gleasie Leatherbury, Annapolis, Maryland, c. 1935, 12½". Collection of the authors.

The green print is a typical feed sack print from the era. All the patches are whip-stitched with white thread.

This is a great example of naive, unpretentious applique design.

outside the upper classes, "life" meant "work." Most of the food was grown, stored and prepared at home. Much of the bedding and clothing was homemade. Families were larger than today, even with the much higher infant mortality of the times. We all know how much flowers can cheer and raise our flagging spirits today – think how wonderful they must have seemed 150 years ago! And tulips must have been a welcome sight in the spring and early summer after a long, relatively colorless winter.

We have talked a great deal about the colors red and green and how they were used in old applique quilts. This is straightforward enough, but **why** those colors were used is more difficult to say.

In the first place, there is the obvious reason to use those, the colors of roses and tulips themselves. New roses are as varicolored and delicately or richly shaded as paint chips. The "classic" rose, however, was – and still is, according to Joe's father – red. The same could be said for tulips. While these patterns developed, in the early 1800's, it was only natural for quiltmakers to seek red and green fabrics to use.

Before 1810 green cloth was only printed by "over-printing" blue and yellow, and even after the first "solid" green was developed that year, overprinting continued for decades. Now, much of the overprinted blue has faded, leaving a yellowish green. But a few years after the first solid green dye was invented, another, even more reliable, appeared. The new green dye was one of a group used in making "oiled," or "oil boiled," cotton, which was more colorfast than earlier dyes, and so called for the step of the dying process which involved soaking the cloth in oil.

The most famous of the new colors was "Turkey Red," named for the near east region where the process was invented. It is that rich, saturated red which often looks brand new on otherwise faded and worn quilts. The process was introduced to this country in 1829, and within a few years "oiled" red, green and yellow were widely available.

Being new, colorfast and already in demand, prints and solids of these colors quickly became fashionable. In *Quilts: Their Story and How to Make Them*, Marie Webster quotes Miss Bessie Daingerfield, a "Kentuckian who has written interestingly of her experiences with mountain quiltmakers," on the subject of applique ("patch") quilts and the fabrics used in them:

"... The colours used are commonly oil red, oil green

18. Tulip and Blue Birds, maker unknown, Indiana, c. 1933, 11". Collection of the authors.

"The tulip was standing pretty in the garden urn. It needed only the birds to complete the first block of the new Nancy Page garden quilt. And here's the bird – a saucy one."

This was the introduction to this first in a 20 block series published in 1932-33. The syndicated column was called "The Nancy Page Quilt Club," and the idea was that by the time the blocks had all been published, readers would have had the time to make them all. The name of the quilt was GARDEN BOUQUET. See pattern section. For examples of the finished quilt, see Texas Quilt, Texas Treasures, *page 127, or* Michigan Quilts, *#144. (See pattern #22.)*

and a certain rather violent yellow, and sometimes indigo blue. These and only these are considered reliable enough for a patch quilt, which is made for the generations that come after."

Some dyes proved not to be reliable at all. Greens sometimes turned tan. Brown or black figures printed on red, green or yellow backgrounds sometimes caused the fabric upon which they were printed to deteriorate, leaving small holes in place of the original stars or sprigs or dots.

Synthetic dyes, invented in 1856, broadened the available palette of colors, but by then red and green was firmly established as the chief color combination for applique quilts. In other words, by the middle of the century, it had become customary to use those colors – together with bits of pink, yellow and blue – for applique quilts, and it took an act of will to use others.

These factors, we think, combined to produce the tradition of red and green appliques:

1. For those inventive women devising the block-style, floral applique quilt, it seemed natural to use the colors of roses and tulips.
2. New dyes became available which made red and green more colorfast, and more desirable for applique quilts.
3. As the demand for those colors increased, so did the supply.
4. The novelty of the patterns and colors led to a fad, or fashion, in quiltmaking.
5. The fashion became a "tradition," so that rose and tulip patterns were customarily "done that way."

By the turn of the 20th century, fashions and customs had changed. The Machine Age brought even more colors to the fabric industry, and new color schemes quickly replaced the old. Writing in 1929, Ruth Finley – a sincere lover of old quilts if ever there was one – betrayed her own 20th century sensibilities when she discussed a 19th century quilt in her book, *Old Patchwork Quilt*. "The green-red-lemon-orange combination," she writes, "Is enough to set a blind man's teeth on edge." Carlie Sexton, a contemporary of Finley's, reinforces this rejection of the old color schemes in her 1930 book, *Yesterday's Quilts in Homes of Today*, when she quotes a character named Phoebe, from the book *Patchwork*, "I don't like this patchin' and I for certain don't like red and green quilts." Sexton goes on, "Red, green, and orange were the most common colors; but vivid as they have been we find some that have softened into the lighter shades that blend with our furnishings . . ."

Pastels had become dominant in home furnishings, so it was no wonder that red and green quilts seemed jarring to the women of the 20's and 30's. By the time quilts began to be made and noticed again in the late 1960's, red

20. Tulip Lady Finger, by the authors, 1987, 6″. Collection of the authors.

We reduced the 1928 Ladies Art Company 15″ block to 6″. Most pieced floral patterns we have seen were designed in this century. (See pattern #23.)

19. Tulip in Vase, maker unknown, Lancaster, Pennsylvania, c. 1860, 17½″. Collection of the authors.

The applique is whip-stitched with white thread. The stems were cut on the straight instead of the bias.

This is an original interpretation of a common design formula of the period.

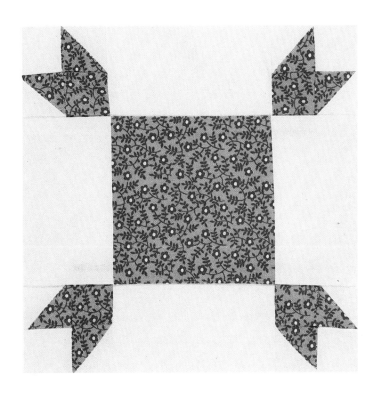

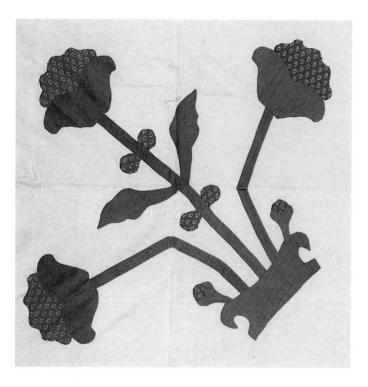

21. Tulip Pot, maker unknown, collected in Pennsylvania, c. 1840-80, 30″. Collection of the authors.

The red parts were whip-stitched with white thread, but the green was done with green thread. Probably an original design, this block seems to us to show the joy and spontenaity of an experienced, skilled needleworker working for pleasure.

and green together had come to symbolize Christmas only. We are so accustomed to this pairing of the color scheme with Christmas that, no matter what time of year it is, when we show people a red and green quilt we expect their first reaction to be, "That would make a wonderful Christmas quilt!" This makes it unlikely that red and green quilts will become generally fashionable again any time soon.

We do not mean to imply that red and green are the only colors we think are proper or enjoy using for rose or tulip quilts. We use blues, browns, oranges, yellows and pinks as well. One example of an alternate color scheme is tan and pink, like we used for our CROSSED TULIPS, Plate 23.

We mentioned that greens sometimes faded to tan. Examine the seams of some old red and tan quilts and you will find evidence that the tan was formerly green. We have seen some quilts, however, that show no evidence that the tan was originally green. In fact, we think some tans were tan. Some browns were brown. We do not know why a quiltmaker might have used tan instead of the more customary green. Perhaps green was not available when she needed it, so she substituted. Perhaps she could not afford new green fabric, so she used the scraps she had on hand.

The old CLEVELAND TULIP in Plate 22 is extremely worn, and it is possible that its tan was formerly green, but in the seams we can find a much darker, brownish tan which appears to have been the original color. In any case, we have found that we like this and other color schemes whether or not they were original.

Today we can stay in touch with each other in the quilt community to the extent that we can hear about new ideas or techniques almost as soon as they are introduced. We have magazines, books, even television shows through which we can be informed. It can be exhilerating to see and try a new idea, and to see the results of others' experiments. One effect of the media on current quiltmaking, though, is the elimination of regional styles. The more we stay in touch across the country and even around the world, the more our quilts look alike.

In the last century, however, quilters were much more isolated. Some never left the communities in which they were born. Without published patterns or organized, nationwide quilt groups, each quiltmaker was on her own to devise solutions to technical or aesthetic problems, which made for diverse and individual quilts.

Of course, some customs **were** widespread, such as color schemes and some design habits. It was common to use white thread for applique, even when colored thread was available. Until 1860 or so, it was common to make leaves diamond-shaped, instead of realistically curved. It was common to make rose and tulip quilts with four large blocks, often a yard square.

22. Tulip Wheel, by Mary Schafer, 1967, 12″. Collection of Cuesta Benberry.

Mary received this pattern in a 1960's block exchange from June Stegina, Hartford, Connecticut. It is June's original design.

Still, within those common approaches were many unique touches, invented as the need or the whim arose. Stems, which we take for granted as going under the flower they support, sometimes went over it. Outline quilting sometimes outlines the **inside** of a shape, instead of the outside. We have already mentioned the unfettered vines that wind around some of our favorite old quilts, but swags were sometimes just as unruly. Individual motif applique borders were so numerous and varied as to defy categorization. Some appear to have been intended as leaves or branches; others seem like small fleur-de-lis. But we do not know if some designs were meant to represent anything. What, for example, was the creature-like shape on the LEE'S ROSE AND BUDS border in Plate 5 supposed to represent?

When we look at old rose or tulip quilts, we often see these sorts of incomprehensible touches. Rather than think, "I could never get away with that today," we try to think, "I wonder how I can use that on my next quilt?"

Windblown Tulip, Pillowslip, maker unknown, Lancaster, Pennsylvania, c. 1920, 19¼″ x 29″. Collection of the authors.

This pattern was copyrighted by Marie Webster and shown in a completed quilt on page 134 of her 1915 book, *Quilts: Their Story and How To Make Them. The Mountain Mist catalogue still offers a similar pattern today. Quiltmakers have long made pillowslips, shams and other accessories to match their quilts.*

Tulip Hand Towels, maker unknown, collected in St. James, Michigan, c. 1930-50. Collection of William and Barbara Cruickshank.

These machine-appliqued hand towels were probably made from a commercial pattern, and they show what happened with applique in this century. Appliqued tulips slipped out of the bedroom and into the kitchen, the dining and living rooms, but not yet into the galleries.

Daffodil and Butterfly, Grapes and Vines, Morning Glory, quilt patterns by Marie D. Webster, Marion, Indiana, 1915-26. Collection of Mary and Fred Schafer.

These three patterns were purchased from Marie Webster sometime in the 1920's by the late Betty Harriman of Bunceton, Missouri. The copyright dates range from 1915 to 1926. The patterns are now in the collection of Mary Schafer.

Printed on brown envelopes is, "Marie D. Webster's The New Quilt Patterns *Marion, Indiana. Price 50 cents." Each envelope has a set of instructions for the quilt, fabric color swatches, a blueprint of the template shapes and, most remarkably, full-size tissue paper models of the applique. The patterns are beautiful objects. Each tissue paper flower and vine is carefully pasted into exact position by hand. They demonstrate an artistic awareness and a commercial savvy distinctly new to quiltmaking.*

These patterns show Marie Webster's efforts to design a new, artful type of applique for the 20th century. All the shapes are stylized, but quite realistic – not crudely abstracted as some of the previous century were. The colors are all new, all solid – not the distracting calicoes of the past. Even the quilting is carefully described in the instructions: "Do not quilt across any leaves, buds, flowers or stems, but around them, this gives the raised effect." In other words, do not quilt right across the applique as did many older quilters.

Ms. Webster was a superb designer, educated and skilled, whose patterns were technically demanding and beautiful. Notice, for example, the thin bias strips that form all the vines. By selling these detailed patterns she could influence many novice quiltmakers who had no previous experience in the craft and give them the complete instructions they needed.

By making artful, symmetrical designs, wholly original and well executed, and by commercializing her work, Marie Webster became the prototypical "quilt professional" of the century. One of the few in her time who had any commercial success, she paved the way for generations of quilt professionals, only a few in the succeeding decades, but appearing in large numbers more than 50 years later.

Gallery

Roses

*"Gorgeous two-toned rose,
Couldn't you decide which color
You wanted to be?"*

Ruby Deardorff Rochelle

Plate 1. BIRTHDAY ROSE made by Gwen Marston for Joe Cunnigham's birthday, 1986, 74″ x 71″. Collection of the authors.

Gwen designed and made this quilt expressly to include some of our favorite features: large-scale pattern on large blocks, free placement of shapes, three-sided border. The quilting is simple diagonals and outline quilting.

This is Joe's sixth birthday quilt from Gwen.

Plate 2. CROSS-STITCH ROSE, top made by Helen Day in Flint, Michigan, in 1952 and completed by Mary Schafer in 1986, 80″ x 97″. Collection of Mary and Fred Schafer.

Mary bought and finished this top so she would have an example of the cross-stitched quilt kits that became popular in the late 40's and early 50's. We have seen many similar pieces – most, like this, unfinished.

The kit for this quilt was purchased through Better Homes and Gardens *magazine around 1950. Helen Day worked on the cross-stitching during her lunch breaks while she worked at an automotive supply factory.*

# of Quilts

Plate 3. DEMOCRATIC ROSE, begun by Betty Harriman © 1960, finished by Mary Schafer, 1981, 80″ x 95″. Collection of Mary and Fred Schafer.

Betty traced the block design from an antique Democratic Rose block she collected. Mary received the antique block, four 30″ appliqued blocks and fabric for the rest of the top. She set the blocks together, designed the center applique and the quilting.

The only reason this was called "Democratic" instead of "Whig" was the political persuasion of the original seamstress.

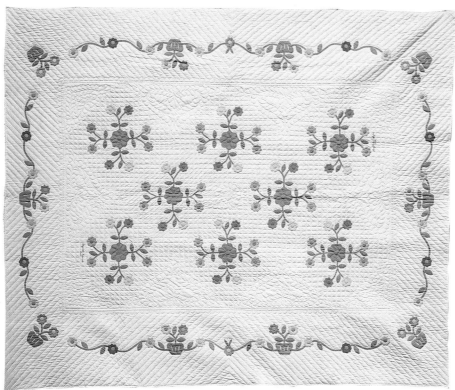

Plate 4. DEMOCRATIC ROSE, begun by Betty Harriman, c. 1923, finished by Mary Schafer, 1979, 83″ x 101″. Collection of Mary and Fred Schafer.

This DEMOCRATIC ROSE bears the imprint of the era in which it was begun. the pastel colors, the "pretty" 20th century style applique border design, the overall cuteness and sweetness are typical of the period when quilts were first revived as nostalgia items. We speculate that its "lightness" may have been the reason Betty lost interest and never completed it.

Plate 5. LEE'S ROSE AND BUDS, begun by Betty Harriman, 1969, finished by Mary Schafer in 1972, 84" x 101". Collection of Mary and Fred Schafer.

Mary received this as a complete quilt top partially marked for the quilting. Betty's notes were attached to the top:

"History 'Rose and Buds' . . . made in 1852 by mother and Grandmother of cousin Mamie Lee – Mamie Lee was born 1860 the night Abraham Lincoln was elected president . . . Quilt now owned by Robert E. Lee, son of Mamie Lee – This quilt is large This old quilt is in perfect condition and very beautiful."

Notable details of this quilt include the three-sided border, the distinctly 19th century style quilting in the plain blocks, the colors – chosen to match the (evidently) faded colors of the original quilt. The quilt exemplifies Betty's style, in that she often chose to duplicate original quilts as closely as possible. Mary's version of this pattern, shown next, shows a much different interpretation. (See pattern #2.)

Plate 6. LEE ROSE AND BUDS, made by Mary Schafer, 1972, 81" x 99½". Collection of Mary and Fred Schafer.

Mary was inspired by Betty's pattern to make her own version. It shows her sensibilities as clearly as Betty's showed her own. Mary used fewer blocks, a four-sided border, darker colors, original quilting designs.

One of our favorite touches on these two quilts is the small embroidered embellishment on the rose buds. (See pattern #2.)

Plate 7. MISSOURI ROSE TREE, begun by Betty Harriman, 1966, and finished by Mary Schafer, 1973, 89" x 92". Collection of Mary and Fred Schafer.

A close copy of the Charlotte Jane Whitehill quilt in the Denver Art Museum, this quilt must have presented exactly the kind of challenge Betty most enjoyed. The small bows in the corners, the pink leaf at the base of each "tree" and the tiny, triple leaves atop each tree were Betty's own refinements of the pattern. It is wonderful to picture a virtuoso quiltmaker like her, working on a masterpiece like this, unable to resist the temptation to make an already rich design richer. (See pattern #6.)

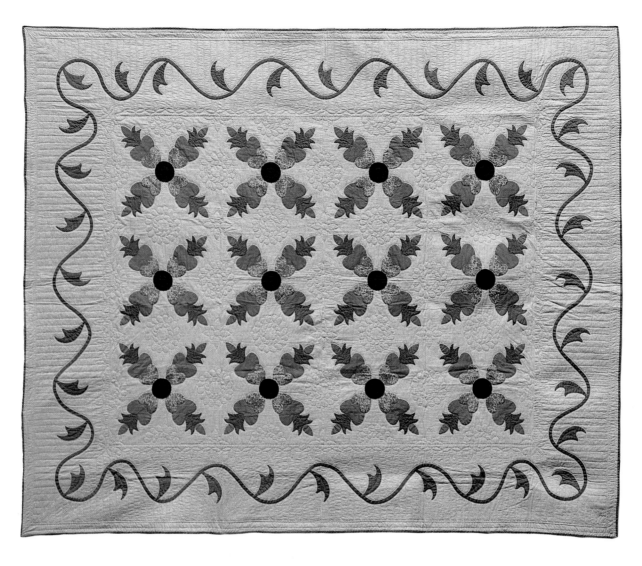

Plate 8. RADICAL ROSE, by Mary Schafer, 1965, 80″ x 97″. Collection of Mary and Fred Schafer.

During the Civil War, quilters put a black circle in the center of this rose as a symbol of their sympathy for the plight of the slaves.

Mary adapted the border design from her SINGLE TULIP, and quilted 5½″ feather wreathes over the seams where the blocks join. Her choice of colors was no doubt influenced by the burgundy and pink combination which was fashionable at the time she made the quilt. (See pattern #8.)

Plate 9. ROSES, blocks by Mary Schafer, set together and quilted by the authors, 1987, 42″ x 42″. Collection of the authors.

Over the years, we have received many quilt blocks from Mary. Often, it seems easier for her to make a block to explain something than to explain it in a letter or telephone conversation. Three of these blocks – Radical Rose, Rose of Sharon and Rose Wreath – appear in other quilts in this book. The fourth, Iowa Rose, is a Nancy Cabot pattern from the 1930's. Together, these four blocks reminded us of a quilt on page 182 of *America's Quilts and Coverlets,* so we used its set and quilting lines. (See patterns #1, #8, #11.)

Plate 10. ROSES AND HEARTS, by Ella McInturff, Mannington, West Virginia, 1963, 82½″ x 98″. Collection of Mary and Fred Schafer.

On a vacation through the South, Fred and Mary spotted a sign that read, "Quilts for Sale." When they stopped to visit, Mary noticed Ella's quilt on her bed, and asked if she would make another one like it.

The colors are typical of the early 60's, the "Ice Cream Cone" border became popular in the 1930's.

Plate 11. ROSES AND HEARTS, by Mary Schafer, 1982, 43½″ x 43½″. Collection of Mary and Fred Schafer.

Mary made this small version of the previous quilt for a 1983 exhibit of her crib and doll quilts at the Citizens Bank Building in Flint, Michigan.

Plate 12. ROSE AND TULIP WREATH, by the authors, 1987, 64½″ x 64½″. Collection of the authors.

Our ideas for this quilt came from a number of quilts – all listed in the reference section. The border was inspired by the border of a four-block quilt shown on page 49 of the 1985 Quilt Digest.

We designed the wreath by tracing around a large bowl. The rounded leaves were cut freehand, others were leftovers from our TULIP VASE AND CHERRIES, plate 40. The borders were made individually before they were added to the quilt. We cut all the shapes from scraps, adding and moving shapes as we worked.

For us, this quilt was a liberating, happy project. Mary has told us many times that she would not enjoy working so loosely, that she could not allow herself to leave the unresolved borders or the crude shapes unrefined. But she likes looking at the quilt as much as we liked making it.

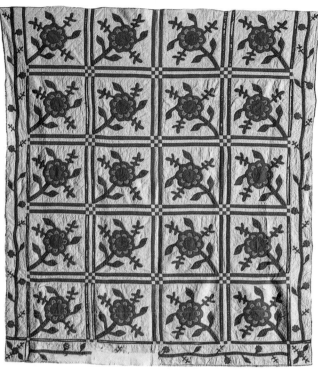

Plate 13. ROSE OF SHARON, maker unknown, c. 1875, 74″ x 79″. Collection of Mary and Fred Schafer.

This old, worn applique quilt, purchased at a thrift store, shows a difficult yet naive approach to design. We think it is the earthy, free quality of the shapes that lends the quilt its charm.

The border leaves, for example, are irregular and crudely shaped, but tiny: ¼″ wide and 1″ long, outline quilted both inside and out.

We liked the pieced lattice so well we used it on our own SINGLE TULIP.

Plate 14. ROSE OF SHARON, by Mary Schafer, 1979, 79″ x 99½″. Collection of the authors.

Mary combined elements from different ROSE OF SHARON quilts in her design for this quilt she made as a gift for Gwen. Mary rarely buys fabric for her quilts, as she has such a vast scrap collection. Even for this elegant quilt she used scraps she had on hand. When she saw that she was running out of the green she was using for the original border, she introduced another, similar green in the corners.

The quilting designs are original, and typical of Mary's graceful, feather-like designs. Notice, too, her typical quilted grid, which moves diagonally against the blocks, drawing them together into a large field by de-emphasizing the piecing lines between them. (See pattern #11.)

Plate 15. ROSE OF SHARON, machine appliqued, hand quilted by the authors, 1987, 36″ x 36″. Collection of the authors.

The last quilt we made for this book, this crib-size ROSE OF SHARON represents our biggest step backward in design and technique. All the shapes were freehand cut, without sketches or patterns – most from folded fabric – and machine appliqued in the style of some of our favorite old machine appliques. The quilting was either freehand, freehand drawn or derived by tracing around cookie cutters.

We did the machine applique by simply basting the seam allowances under, pinning the pieces in place and top-stitching them along the very edge with a straight stitch, 18 stitches to the inch. We started and stopped in the same place and pulled all thread ends through to the back, weaving them into the body of the quilt.

Plate 16. ROSE WREATH, maker unknown, c. 1850, collected in Fayetteville, Pennsylvania, 76″ x 76″. Collection of Mary and Fred Schafer.

The wreath of this worn applique runs in a complete circle beneath the roses; the mustard-yellow center of each rose was reverse appliqued. The diagonal quilting lines are ½″ apart and form a tight grid where they cross in the middle of each block.

Working with Mary when we prepared this book, we were all taken with this classic wreath pattern, so much so that reproducing it is one of Mary's current projects.

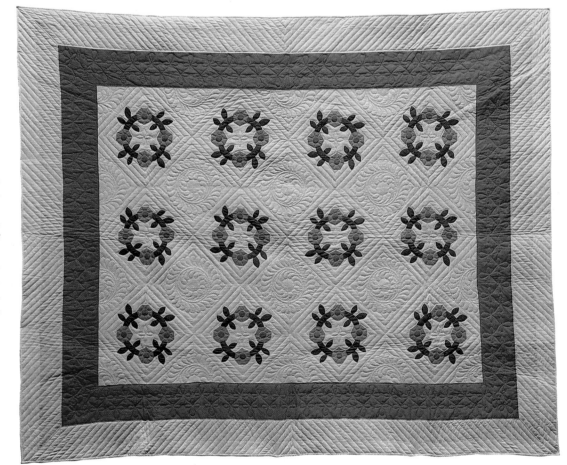

Plate 17. ROSE WREATH, top begun c. 1930-40, maker unknown, Shipshewana, Indiana, completed by Mary Schafer, 1985, 75″ x 95″. Collection of Mary and Fred Schafer.

This top shows the era in which it was made, with its straight-sided seven-point flowers, its colors and its wide inner border.

Plate 18. WASHINGTON ROSE, begun by Betty Harriman, 1969, completed by Mary Schafer, 1984, 90½″ x 92″. Collection of Mary and Fred Schafer.

Mary took this pattern from a quilt she saw at "My Old Kentucky Home" in Bardstown, Kentucky. The historical home was built by Judge John Rowan and is now a state park. When she sent the pattern to Betty, Betty wrote to tell her how happy she was to have a pattern from the home, especially because Judge Rowan was one of her ancestors.

Betty completed one quilt of this pattern and started this one before she died. Mary appliqued the unusual and handsome border design. (See pattern #12.)

Plate 19. WHIG ROSE, maker unknown, c. 1850, Greenfield, Massachusetts, 104″ x 106″. Collection of Mary and Fred Schafer.

The center rose was completely pieced before it was whip stitched to the ground over the shapes already in place. Yellow circles were reverse appliqued in the center of each red rose. The appliqued patches are all outline quilted both inside and out. Leaves, single flowers and various floral sprays are quilted into all the avaialble white spaces, except the outer border, which has a dense grapes, vine and leaf quilting pattern. The edges of the quilt are turned inward and top-stitched with a treadle machine.

The freehand quilting, free placement of the applied patches, the delicate bias work – all suggest a confident, expert needleworker finding her own solutions to design problems.

Plate 20. WHIG ROSE, maker unknown, c. 1850, West Chester, Pennsylvania, 89″ x 90″. Collection of Mary and Fred Schafer.

The colors and the boldness of this rose pattern are exemplary of Pennsylvania German quilts of this period. Its thin, flannel batting and the tiny calico prints make it difficult to make out the quilting, even from 6″ away. The four blocks have simple cross-hatching, the inner border has a zig-zag and the outer border has an eight-strand cable. The unusual aspect of the quilting is that it was done with thread that matched the color of the background, rare among 19th century quilts.

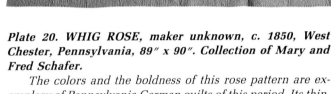
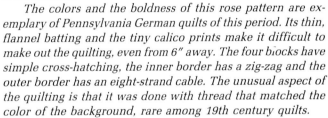

Plate 21. WHIG ROSE, maker unknown, c. 1850, West Chester, Pennsylvania, 89″ x 90″. Collection of Mary and Fred Schafer.

Mary acquired this quilt and the previous one from the same dealer at the same time. When we first saw them, we thought they might have been made by the same quiltmaker, but in studying them for this book we realized they use much different techniques and are significantly different in style.

The batting here is very thick, but that did not prevent the maker from doing elaborate quilting designs with tiny stitches. It has feather wreaths, hearts, pineapples, pinwheels, leaves, rosettes, cross-hatching and diagonals. All the applique is outline quilted inside and out.

This is one of the few quilts we studied for this book which had mitered corners. Twenty-five-inch-width fabric was pieced to make the thirty-three-inch square foundation blocks.

Comparing these three WHIG ROSE quilts we can see the truth in the statement an older quilter made to Dorothy Cozart during her research: "We didn't name them, we just made them."

Tulips

"Clean as a lady,
Cool as glass
Fresh without fragrance
the tulip was."

Humbert Wolfe

Plate 22. CLEVELAND TULIP, maker unknown, c. 1860, 86″ x 89″. Collection of the authors.

We found this tattered masterpiece in a thrift store in Galesburg, Illinois, for one dollar. It has snaps sewn to one edge, probably by its last owner, who most likely used it as a mattress pad. In spite of its sad condition, it has all the attributes of applique quilts we most admire: original ideas freely executed.

The tulip is one of many floral designs based on the eight-pointed star. The alternate blocks were appliqued with a design we have not seen elsewhere. The center block is a variation of the alternate block design. The appliqued border is made of four elaborate corner vines that meet in the middle of each side, each vine made of one piece of bias tape that tapers from ¾″ at the corner to ⅛″ at the base of the bud at the end.

All the quilting seems to have been done freehand – echo quilting, outline quilting, diagonals, flowers and leaves. The entire quilt is restrained, calm, dignified and effortless.

Plate 23. CROSSED TULIPS, by the authors, 1987, 71″ x 72″. Collection of the authors.

Inspired by faded wonders like the CLEVELAND TULIP, the many crossed tulip variations and, for the pink-tipped leaves, a sampler quilt shown in the 1987 Quilt Art Engagement Calendar, (#41), we made this tulip especially for this book.

We derived the pattern by sketching the shapes on paper and tracing the tulip at the window to make it symmetrical. Because we wanted the placement of the shapes to be fairly regular, we creased the foundation blocks corner to corner to help us position them.

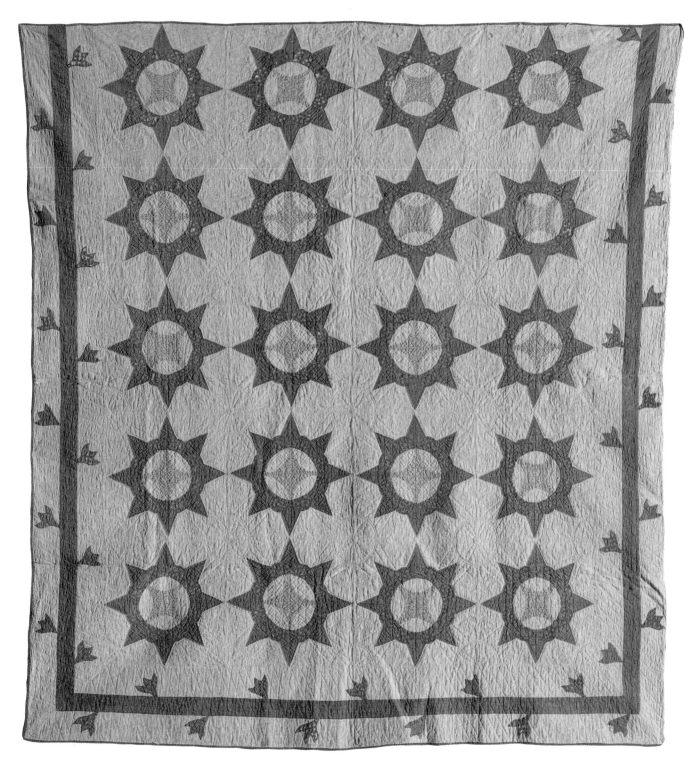

Plate 24. FULL BLOWN TULIP, made by a member of the Parshall family, Saginaw, Michigan, c. 1850, 72″ x 87″. Collection of Mary and Fred Schafer.

Slight variations of this pattern are sometimes called "Rose Album," "Ceasar's Crown" and other names. Mary Schafer says she thinks the pattern may have been inspired by looking straight down on a completely open tulip.

Most pieced floral patterns were developed during this century – this is one of the few which were common during the last.

Plate 25. GIANT TULIP, by the authors, 1980, 70″ x 80″. Collection of the authors.

We copied this quilt from a tattered old quilt on page 194 of American Quilts and Coverlets, by Safford and Bishop (#290).

The small black and white photo of the original showed that it had everything we look for in quilts: interesting quilting, bold shapes, eccentricity. After many conversations with Mary Schafer about the quilt, speculating on the colors, studying the quilting, thinking about what kind of quilter might have made it, Mary drafted a pattern and started a copy of the quilt the same week we did.

This was the first time we used the fan quilting design that we came to use often in later quilts. Using the design here made us notice how many old appliques were quilted with lines right across the appliqued shapes. Also, it opened our eyes to the often used freehand fan design – where the quilter judged the concentric arcs by eye, with no markings.

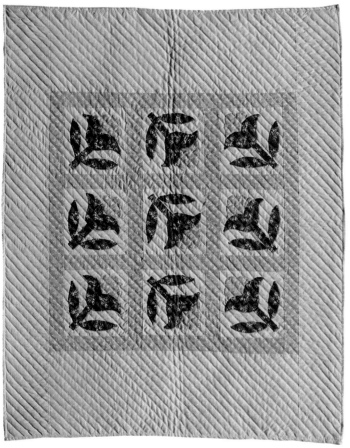

Plate 26. GWEN'S TULIP, by the authors, 1983, 41″ x 33½″. Collection of the authors.

Gwen designed this pattern as a beginner's project for an applique class she taught at a Flint, Michigan, high school. The simple diagonal quilting lines imitate those sometimes marked on old quilts by snapping a chalk line diagonally across the quilt top. (See pattern #14.)

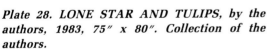

Plate 27. HOLLAND QUEEN, begun by Betty Harriman, 1965, completed by Mary Schafer, 1978, 83″ x 99″. Collection of Mary and Fred Schafer.

Betty made the blocks; Mary designed the applique border and the quilting.

According to Betty's notes, "This pattern came from the Netherlands." It is a strong example of the balanced, meticulous type of work at which both these quiltmakers excel. (See pattern #15.).

Plate 28. LONE STAR AND TULIPS, by the authors, 1983, 75″ x 80″. Collection of the authors.

Inspired by a number of Lone Star and Tulip patterns, (see the reference section,) we modeled the center of this quilt after a crib quilt shown on page 33 of Crib Quilts and Other Small Wonders.

Roses and tulips were often used to embellish pieced quilts like this. Some quiltmakers, it appears, were unable to resist the lure of a large, empty space calling for applique.

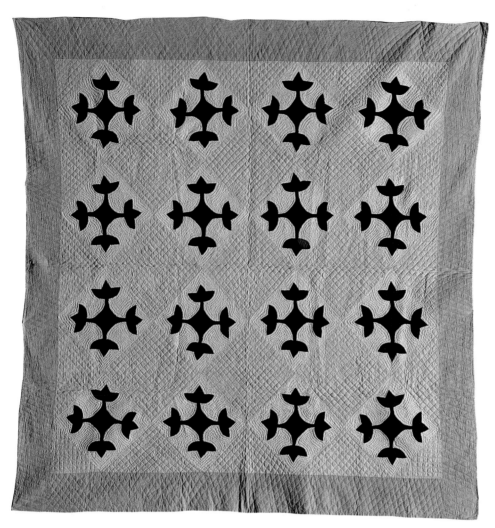

Plate 29. MRS. EWER'S TULIP, maker unknown, "Ellie" quilted into one block and underlined with brown thread, collected in Gettysburg, Pennsylvania, c. 1850-75, 85" x 86". Collection of Mary and Fred Schafer.

All the applique is whip-stitched with white thread; the brown applique is quilted with brown thread and the green tulips with green thread. The echo quilting, cross-hatching and hanging diamond pattern on the border are quilted in white.

This seems like a "country" quilt, with its slightly irregular shapes, cottonseed-filled batting and possibly homedyed green and brown fabric. Nevertheless, the signature and the fine condition of this old quilt indicate that it may have been intended for "best" use.

Plate 30. PENNSYLVANIA DUTCH FLOWER GARDEN, begun by Betty Harriman, date unknown, completed by Mary Schafer, 1973, 81" x 103". Collection of Mary and Fred Schafer.

These 12 blocks and 13 others were first published by Country Gentleman in 1941 in an article about a sampler quilt from 1850. Around 1945, Charlotte Jane Whitehill used all of the patterns in her famous BRIDE'S QUILT, now in the Denver Art Museum.

Few applique samplers of the 19th century failed to include either roses, tulips or both, like this one. Betty made some of the blocks and had patterns for the others. Mary made the rest of the blocks and designed the border and quilting. The pattern for the tulip wreath block is given in the pattern section, #24.

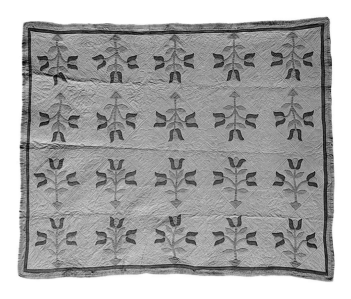

Plate 31. SINGLE TULIP, maker unknown, collected in Salem, Michigan, c. 1860, 69″ x 97″. Collection of Mary and Fred Schafer.

This is exactly the type of everyday applique which we have tried to learn about and imitate. It is not showy or intricate, but a straightforward design statement as appealing to us as analogous pieced designs. Pieced quilts are often admired **for** their simplicity, but appliques like this rarely are.

Plate 32. SINGLE TULIP, by a member of the Lintner family, Hamilton, Ohio, c. 1850, 82″ x 82″. Collection of Mary and Fred Schafer.

This is the border design Mary adapted for her RADICAL ROSE. All the applique is whip-stitched with white thread except the green-stitched leaves. The tulips are pieced, and they were sewn down before the stems. The stems extend over the tulips, folded into a neat point. Instead of outline quilting around each patch, the double diagonals go right to the edge of the applique and the outline quilting is on the inside of each patch.

The rest of the quilting consists of full and half feather wreaths and cross-hatching. The border diagonals change directions freely, or clumsily, whichever you prefer to call it. We think this quilt was made for "best," given its condition and the attention paid to its details.

Plate 33. SINGLE TULIP, by the authors, 1985, 68″ x 82″. Collection of the authors.

This was one of 13 quilts we made for an exhibit called "Now and Then," which paired our quilts with 13 of Mary Schafer's which we had used for inspiration. While our main idea was to make a new SINGLE TULIP which indeed had **one** tulip instead of the usual three, we eventually combined elements from many quilts.

First, we used an old fashioned set with half and quarter blocks. Then came the pieced lattice from Mary's old ROSE OF SHARON (Plate 13,) the chunky inside border from an old quilt shown in our book, Sets and Borders, (page 23) several green and red fabrics as we ran out of each one, brown thread when we ran out of matching thread, a freely designed applique border and freehand-drawn feather quilting. The tulip pattern is the same as GWEN'S TULIP, Plate 26. (See pattern #14.)

Plate 34. SMITHSONIAN TULIP, by the authors, 1983, 77″ x 97″. Collection of the authors.
We found this pattern in an article by Cuesta Benberry in the summer, 1972 issue of Nimble Needle Treasures.
*The article is about a Smithsonian-owned quilt of this pattern with fancier set and border designs. The pattern
seems almost medieval in character, stark and "folky."*

*With Mary's permission, we used her quilting design from the ROSE OF SHARON in Plate 14 for the in-
terior. Appliqued swags might have been appropriate for the borders, but we chose to use quilted swags. (See
pattern #18.)*

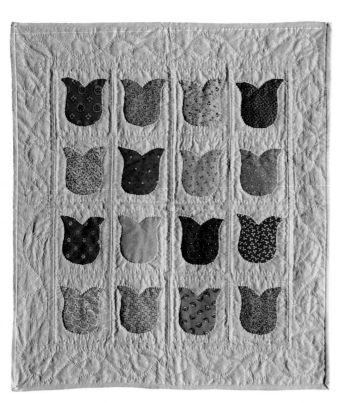

Plate 35. TULIP, by Gwen Marston, 1985, 19″ x 17″. Collection of the authors.

Exploring tulip designs, it was natural for Gwen to try this reduction to the simplest of all tulip shapes. This doll quilt was an excuse to use a few scraps of our favorite, out of print fabrics in a "charm" format, where all the pieces are different.

Fairfield Processing Corporation used this quilt and its pattern for a free pattern included with their polyester batts in 1987.

Plate 36. TULIP, maker unknown, c. 1930, 59″ x 77″. Collection of the authors.

This quilt was a gift to us from Merry Silber, who knew of our interest in primitive tulip patterns. She said, "As soon as I saw this I knew you would love it." She was right.

The applique and quilting are energetic but wild, and show evidence of several hands at work. Perhaps it was a beginner's project for a group of women, or a mother and daughter.

In any case, the great variation in the shapes, differently interpreted leaves, the freehand quilting – all make for a work of charm and originality.

Once again, this quilt represents the type of piece we discussed in the text: a humble, utility applique quilt which, for us, has as much graphic interest and life as more noted pieced utility quilts. We think quilts like this were often made in the past, but have been nearly eradicated from today's quiltmaking scene.

Plate 37. TULIP, by Gwen Marston and Mary Schafer, 1980, 88″ x 96″. Collection of Gladys and Mendal Miller.

Gwen took this pattern from The Standard Book of Quiltmaking, *by Marguerite Ickis to use for her first applique quilt. Mary Schafer coached her on making the blocks and setting them together, then rewarded her efforts by adding the applique border, (adapted from her quilt in Plate 24,) and designing the quilting.*

This is a fine project for a novice, as it is large and uncomplicated yet intricate enough to require most of the techniques for any applique.

Gwen gave this quilt to her parents for their 50th wedding anniversary.

Plate 38. TULIP AND OAK LEAF, by the authors, 1987, 75″ x 75″. Collection of the authors.

We took the idea for this "folded paper" pattern from a quilt in the 1985 Jeanette Lasansky book, In the Heart of Pennsylvania *(page 39). Searching through our fabrics for suitable, bold colors, we found a piece of orange cotton we once tried to buy from Jeff Gutcheon at his shop.*

"I won't sell you that," he said, and threw it in our bag for free.

Well, it **is** *a little bright. But we used it here because it suited the pattern. We tried to use quilting designs that suited the pattern as well – diagonal lines, feather wreaths and a border cable.*

Plate 39. TULIP POT AND CHERRIES, by the authors, 1987, 66″ x 66″. Collection of the authors.

The loose, "slappy" feeling of this quilt comes from using paper templates, placing the patches without marks, cutting the reverse applique slits freehand and other old-fashioned techniques. We used the sewing machine to piece the three-part tulips before we sewed them down and to machine applique the large, straight stems.

The quilt is completely original, but completely derived from other quilts. The sources for it are too numerous to list. The overall idea, however, came from a short passage in one of our favorite books, Old Patchwork Quilts, *by Ruth Finley. Talking about 4-block applique quilts of the mid-19th century, she says.*

"They saw harder usage than those of small designs, because, taking less time to make, they could be replaced more easily (page 124)."

In other words, she claims that at one time, making this type of quilt was no big deal. This idea, of course, is exactly the opposite of the contemporary thinking about applique: that it is so difficult and demanding that it was, and is, reserved for showpiece quilts.

From Mrs. Finley's statement we have concocted our "No Big Deal" theory. That is, instead of planning, drawing, matching and mapping a quilt ahead of time, it is possible to make quilts with the idea that is is no big deal . . . to make a quilt by choosing some fabric, cutting out some shapes and sewing them down spontaneously.

Plate 40. TULIP SAMPLER, by the authors, 1982-84, 80″ x 95″. Collection of the authors.

There are two main sources for our ideas in this quilt. A Pennsylvania quilt shown in the 1985 Quilt Art Engagement Calendar, #47) inspired us to want to make a red and green sampler, and quilt #30 in the same calendar, boldly signed and titled CENTENNIAL, ave us the idea to sign and name it in large letters.

In 1982, we started making the blocks, using whatever fabrics we had at hand we ran across a pattern we wanted to include. Mary chafer even contributed to our project with a few blocks for a full-size quilt.

Designing the quilt was fairly simple: we simply laid the blocks out on the floor, keeping the heaviest ones in the middle, and, when e had a pleasing arrangement, filled in the spaces with plain or pieced strips. The heaviest proved to be the wheel-like tulip wreath e took from the same source as the patterns in Pennsylvania Dutch Flower Garden, Plate 30. (See pattern #21.) Last, we added borders sides first, then top and bottom – to make the top the size we wanted, leaving space for the letters.

For more information about this quilt and a few of the quilting designs, see our article about random samplers in the March, 1986, adys Circle Patchwork Quilts magazine.

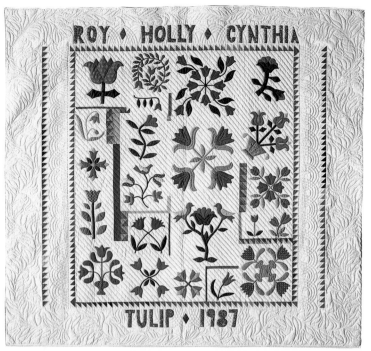

Plate 41. TULIP SAMPLER, by the authors, 1987, 106″ x 96″. Collection of Cynthia and Roy Holly.

Cynthia saw our TULIP SAMPLER at one of our lectures and commissioned us to make one for a surprise 50th wedding anniversary present for her husband, Roy. The Hollys have used tulips extensively in their landscaping, so this was a perfect quilt for them.

For this quilt we took patterns from many sources and even designed a few. Mary Schafer again contributed blocks to the project. The small crossed tulip block was taken from a quilt by Joe's great-grandmother, Minnie Roe. (See pattern #16.) We designed special tulip quilting for the border. Since we never seem to tire of tulips, this quilt was one of our most enjoyable commissions.

Plate 42. TULIP TREE AND BUNNIES, by the authors, 1984, 66″ x 77″. Collection of Matthew Marston. Photo by the authors.

Gwen designed this quilt for her son, Matt, who, as a child, loved bunnies and cherry pies. The tulip tree was machine appliqued but the rest of the applique was done by hand. We quilted it with all-over, freehand fans.

Gwen says, "The quilts I enjoy making most are for the people I love . . . next are the ones I make for myself."

Plate 43. UNCONVENTIONAL TULIP, by the authors, 1984, 82½″ x 82½″. Private collection. Photo by the authors.

Joe designed this quilt by enlarging the block pattern from a quilt called, CONVENTIONAL TULIP in Marie Webster's book, Quilts: Their Story and How To Make Them, (page 79). We made the quilt like a four block quilt, with four square blocks. It is mostly fan quilted. All the stems but the curved ones are pieced.

Plate 44. EAGLE, by the authors, 1986, 79″ x 79″. Collection of the authors.

As we mentioned in our Caption for the LONE STAR, Plate 28, tulips are often used as embellishments for other pieced or appliqued designs. Here, we put a tulip in one eagle's beak. The other eagles have an olive branch, a basket and a firecracker.

The stars and center design were made by folding and cutting fabric freehand. For the shield-shaped bodies, the wings and tails, we made paper templates.

This kind of four-block eagle quilt with an exploding star in the middle was popular in Pennsylvania around the time of the 1876 centennial celebration.

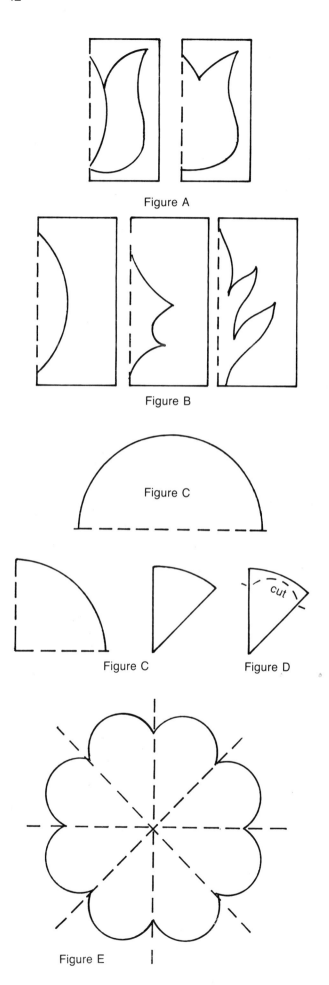

Figure A

Figure B

Figure C

Figure C   Figure D

cut

Figure E

How We

"To applique" means to sew one piece of fabric onto another. In quiltmaking, applique has only a few basic steps: cutting out patches, placing them and sewing them down. Some methods break each of these basic steps down into numerous sub-steps. The process can be made as simple or as complex as you desire. Old quilts show evidence that quilters have always "personalized" their techniques to suit their personalities. Our personalities seem to tend toward the simple, the unrefined, while Mary Schafer's tends towards the rich and highly refined. Oddly, though, we have similar work methods, basically the same as Mary Johnson's and LaVerne Mathews, the quiltmakers we mentioned in the text.

To design our patterns, we sketch on paper the size of our block, tracing against a window when we want something symmetrical; or we cut freehand without a pattern.

We make our own templates by cutting out the shapes from our refined sketch, using either the paper itself for a template, or gluing the shape to cardboard.

We cut our patches with sharp fabric scissors, leaving ¼" all the way around each for a seam allowance and clipping the inside curves of the seam allowance so we can turn it neatly.

To place the shapes on the foundation block, we crease the block from corner to corner and sometimes mark dots for the points of leaves or the top of a shape.

Finally, we pin each piece in place, turn under the edge with our needle and sew it down with a blind stitch.

If our applique pattern includes layering one patch on top of another, we trim out the lower patches to make it possible to quilt through the layers.

Pattern Drafting

As we have said, our techniques are basic and simple. For tulips, we start out with a square of paper the size we want the finished flower or a bit larger. Then we sketch the shape crudely and loosely on the paper. When it is more or less how we want it, we fold the paper in half and refine one half of the flower, then hold the folded paper up to the window and trace the other half. Figure A shows 2 sample tulips, folded at the dotted line for tracing.

We design leaves the same way. Figure B shows leaf shapes, again folded on the dotted line for tracing.

Roses are simple, too. Here are the steps:

1. Cut a circle the same size or a little larger than you want the finished rose.
2. Fold the circle in half three times, as in Figure C.
3. Trace around a coin or other small circle near the end of the "cone," so that both its sides are the same length as in Figure D. Cut on the dotted line.
4. Unfold the paper to find Figure E, the basis of many rose patterns.

Work

For a 6-sided rose shape, start with a circle again, then fold it into thirds, as in Figure F. (Sometimes we use a protractor to find the exact 60 degree fold lines.) Then make a half-circle near the top, as above, so that both sides of the cone are the same length. Cut on the dotted line for Figure G.

Make 8-pointed stars and 6-pointed stars by following the same steps, except cutting the half-circle. Once the circle has been folded into a cone, just fold the point up to the middle of the arc, and trace along both sides to make Figure H.

For our free interpretation of these shapes, we just fold and cut without marking. If we unfold the paper to find we are not happy with the shape, we simply refold and cut again.

Quilting Designs

Quilting designs are less compelling than pieced or appliqued patterns. It is possible to know and love quilts and still to be almost unaware that the stitching which holds them together contains shapes and forms sometimes surpassing the graphic, color design in richness and beauty. Since we first began making quilts as a team, our favorite part of the process has been the hand quilting – sitting at our full-size quilting frame, talking, listening to music or just being quiet. We suggest that those who do not enjoy quilting should find a quilting partner.

Like rose and tulip applique patterns, quilting designs of the last century came in a few major types with much variation and individuality within each category. Many of the designs from long ago are still in use, albeit changed or enlarged, but many have fallen into disuse for some of the same reasons rose and tulip applique patterns have. Few of the quilters pursuing quilts as art are interested in adding feathered plumes to a modern, hard-edged abstraction. It is now thought the quilting should have to do with and support the graphic color design. It need not. Look at the quilts in this book and see how often the quilting goes over the applique or makes a boldly independent statement.

There are three broad categories of quilting designs on the quilts in this book:

1. All-Over Designs . . . diagonals and their variations, (cross-hatching, plaids, hanging diamond, etc.) fans, teacup, clamshell and others. These designs were often used to cover an entire quilt top, sometimes used to fill blocks or borders.
2. Block and Border Designs . . . feathered vines, wreaths or plumes, cables and some all-over designs already mentioned. These designs were used to fill large, well-defined spaces like alternate plain blocks or plain borders.
3. Individual Motifs . . . flowers, leaves, pineapples,

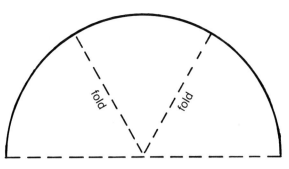

Figure F

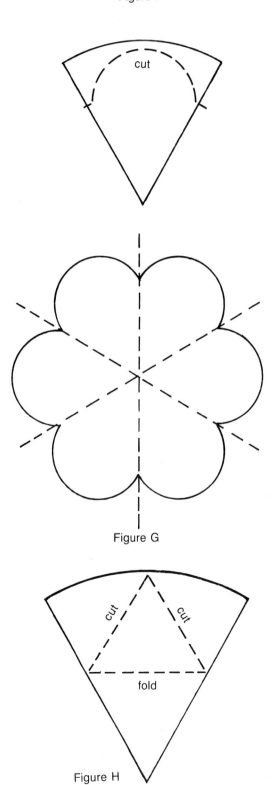

Figure G

Figure H

pinwheels, hearts, hands and others. These designs were used wherever the quilter wanted to fill an odd-shaped empty space between other quilting designs or between applique parts.

A fourth type of quilting had no actual design of its own, but functioned strictly as support for the applique: outline quilting, (sometimes around the **inside** of a shape as well as the outside,) echo quilting and stipple quilting, used to fill areas both small and large, generally between other quilting designs.

Quilters of the last century, like those today, sometimes had a few stencils and knew how to mark a few other designs that they used on all their quilts. Others quilted their designs freehand, giving their quilts a distinctive, eccentric finish.

Our advantage as quilters today is that we can study thousands of quilts from all over the world for ideas. This broad range of options can also paralyze, as it can seem impossible to choose from so many equally effective designs. The way we narrow our range of choices for our quilts is by choosing quilting designs characteristic of those on the quilts we are emulating.

On the TULIP AND CHERRY POT, for instance, we used a common – all **too** common, some might say –

patient work on a quilt top, our tendency is to feel that the quilting is an obstacle that stands between us and our finished quilt. We want to dispense with it as soon as possible. But by giving the quilting as much attention as the applique we can give our quilts as much character and life as possible. Perfunctory quilting – widely spaced, excessively simple – will add nothing to the finished work. Rich, close quilting will more than repay the extra effort it requires. So, even though we are impatient, we usually take our time with the quilting. We are always glad we did.

ROSE OF SHARON

CROSSED TULIPS

TULIP & CHERRY POT

feather wreath, but we placed it so it would extend over the applique. We have seen this technique on many old quilts, few new ones. We felt the machine appliqued ROSE OF SHARON, called for the kind of free, folky design we had seen on similar quilts. The calm, dignified CROSSED TULIPS called for calm, dignified quilting. And so on.

We are often tempted to rush the quilting, as we are impatient to see the finished product once we have completed the applique. It is difficult to slow down and, in effect, start over when we design the quilting. After long,

Pattern Section

All the patterns in this section are from quilts or blocks shown in this book.

The patterns are full-size, listed in alphabetical order within both the rose and tulip sections. The shapes need only to be traced for full-size templates. Remember to allow for seams around all the pattern pieces and foundation blocks.

Most of the blocks are too large to fit on a page, so we used dotted lines to indicate where the pattern should be extended.

Roses

1. **Iowa Rose**, (Plate 9), 18″ finished block.
2. **Lee's Rose and Buds**, (Plates 5 & 6), 13″ finished block, 12½″ border.
3. **Martha Washington Rose**, (Block 1), 10″ finished block.
4. **Mexican Rose**, (Block 2), 18″ finished block.
5. **Michigan Rose**, (Block 3), 12″ finished block.
6. **Missouri Rose Tree**, (Plate 7), 22″ finished block, 12½″ top and bottom borders, 11½″ side borders.
7. **Old English Rose**, (Block 4), 24″ finished block, ⅜″ bias stems.
8. **Radical Rose**, (Plate 8), 18″ finished block, 14″ border, ½″ bias vine.
9. **Rose Wreath**, (Block 7), 12½″ finished block.
10. **Rosebud**, (Block 8), 12″ finished block.
11. **Rose of Sharon**, (Plate 14), 18″ finished block, 11½″ border.
12. **Washington Rose**, (Plate 18), 17″ finished block, 9″ border.

Tulips

13. **Four Tulips**, (Plate 40), 11″ block.
14. **Gwen's Tulips**, (Plates 26 & 33), 6¼″ finished block.
15. **Holland Queen**, (Plate 27), 22″ finished block, 14″ top and bottom borders, 7″ side borders.
16. **Minnie Roe's Tulip**, (Plate 41), 8½″ finished block.
17. **Single Tulip**, (Plate 32), 14½″ finished block, 10¾″ border.
18. **Smithsonian Tulip**, (Plate 34), 18″ finished block.
19. **Tulip**, (Block 14), 12″ finished block.
20. **Tulip**, (Block 15), 12″ finished block.
21. **Tulip**, (Plates 40 & 41), 18″ finished block.
22. **Tulip and Blue Birds**, (Block 18), 11″ finished block.
23. **Tulip Ladyfinger**, (Block 20), 6″ finished block.
24. **Tulip Wreath**, (Plate 30), 18″ finished block.

1. Iowa Rose

2. Lee's Rose and Buds

48

2. Lee's Rose and Buds (Cont.)

3. Martha Washington Rose

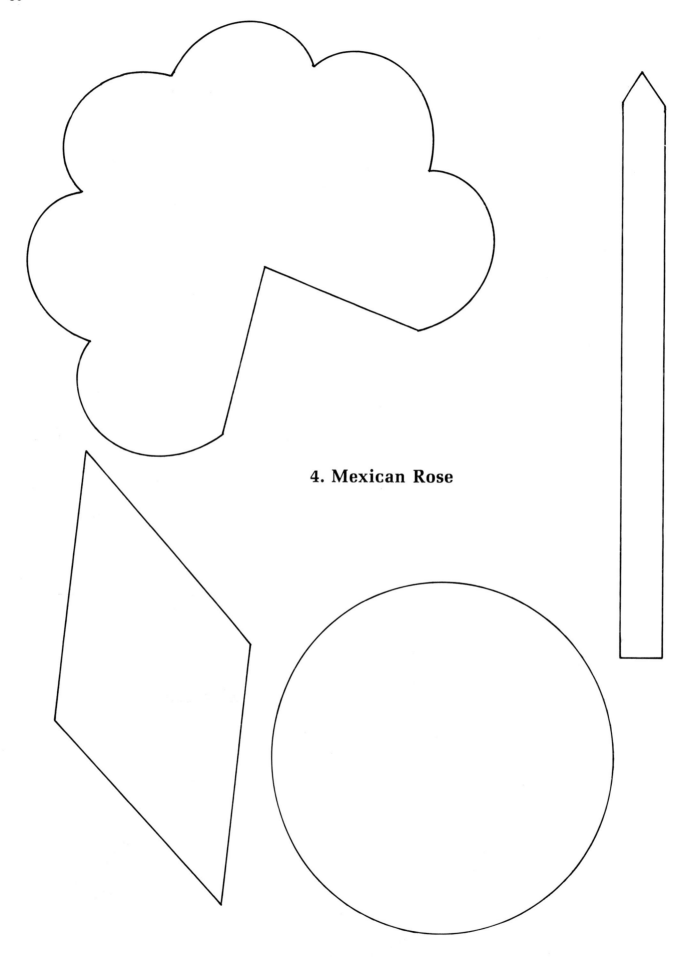

4. Mexican Rose

5. Michigan Rose

52

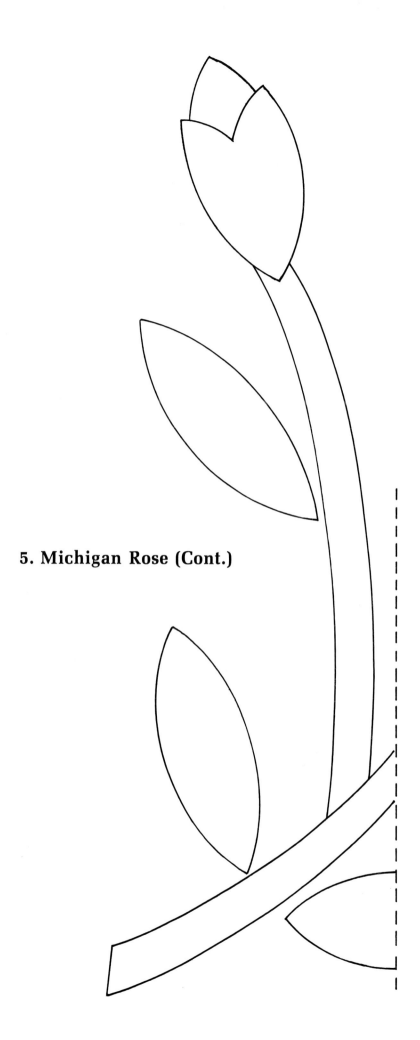

5. Michigan Rose (Cont.)

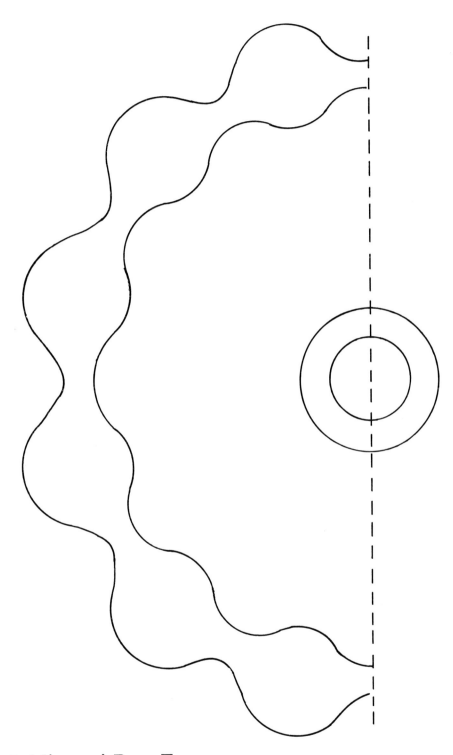

6. Missouri Rose Tree

6. Missouri Rose Tree (Cont.)

6. Missouri Rose Tree (Cont.) Border

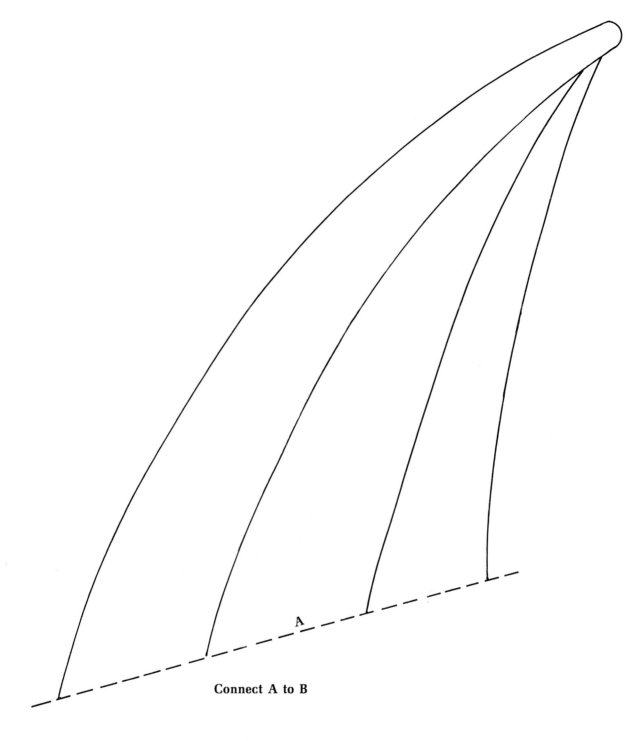

A

Connect A to B

6. Missouri Rose Tree (Cont.) Border

57

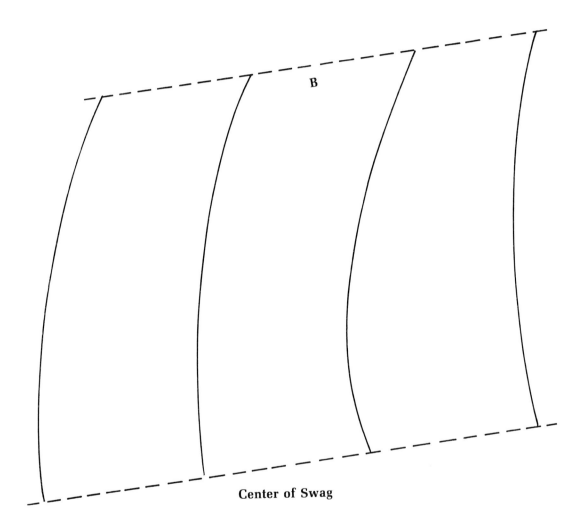

B

Center of Swag

6. Missouri Rose Tree (Cont.) Border

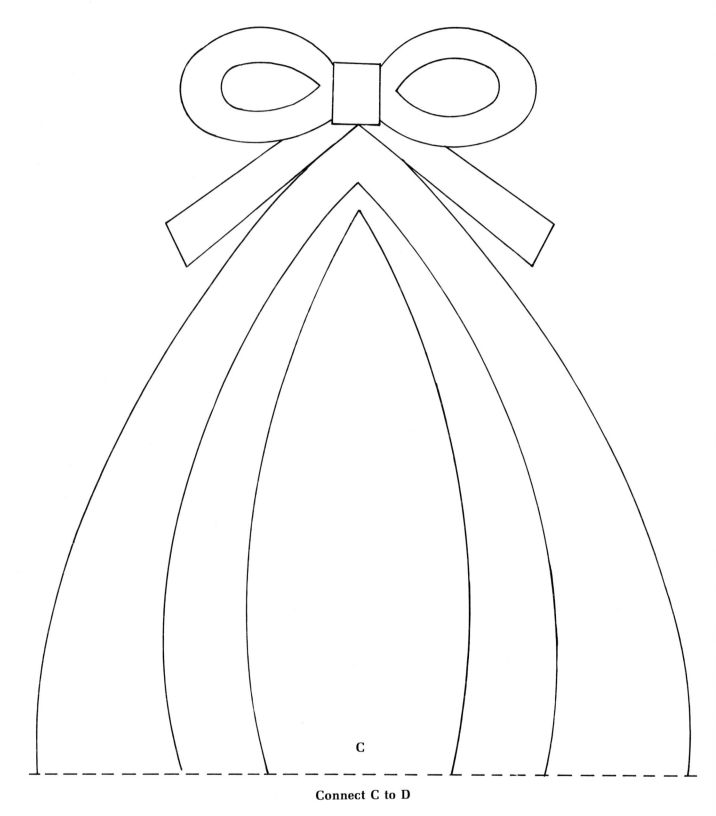

C

Connect C to D

6. Missouri Rose Tree (Cont.) Border

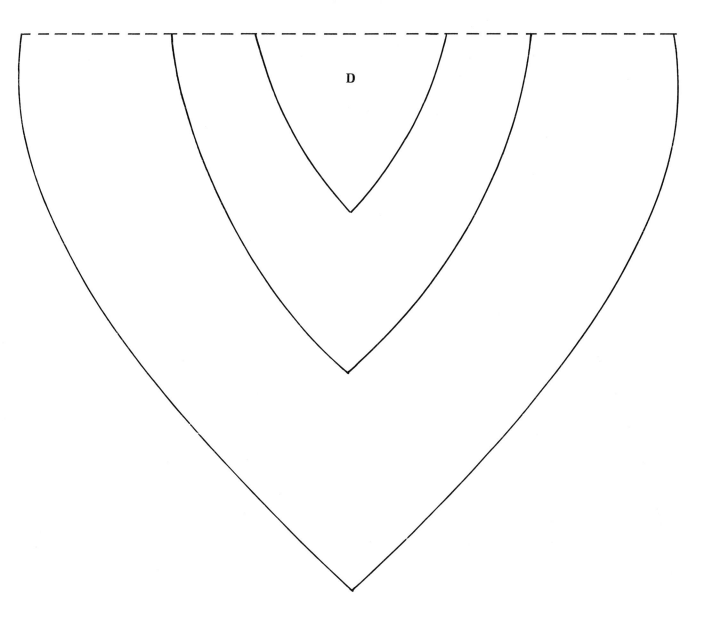

D

6. Missouri Rose Tree (Cont.) Corner

7. Old English Rose

7. Old English Rose (Cont.)

7. Old English Rose (Cont.)

8. Radical Rose

9. Rose Wreath

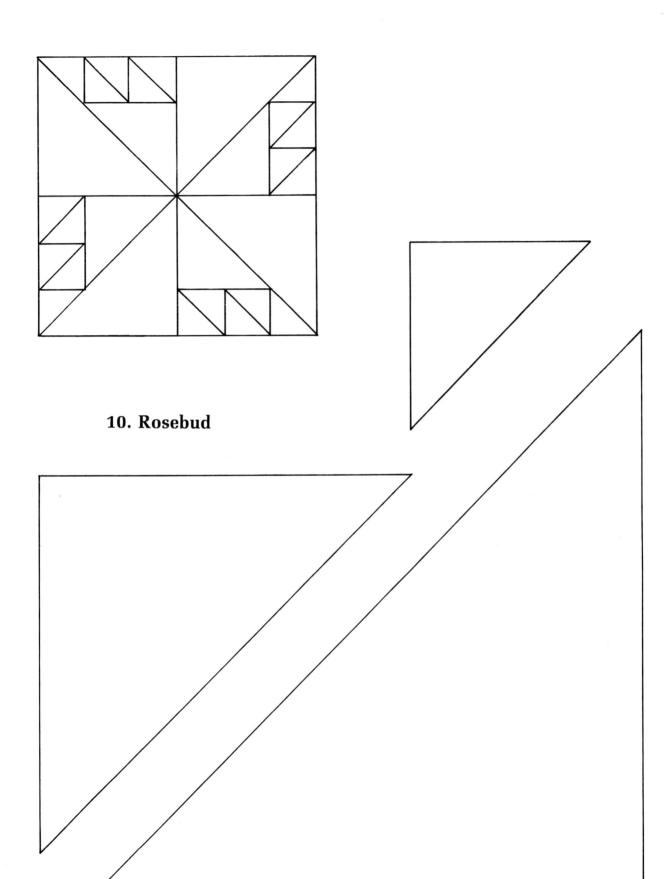

10. Rosebud

11. Rose of Sharon

11. Rose of Sharon (Cont.)

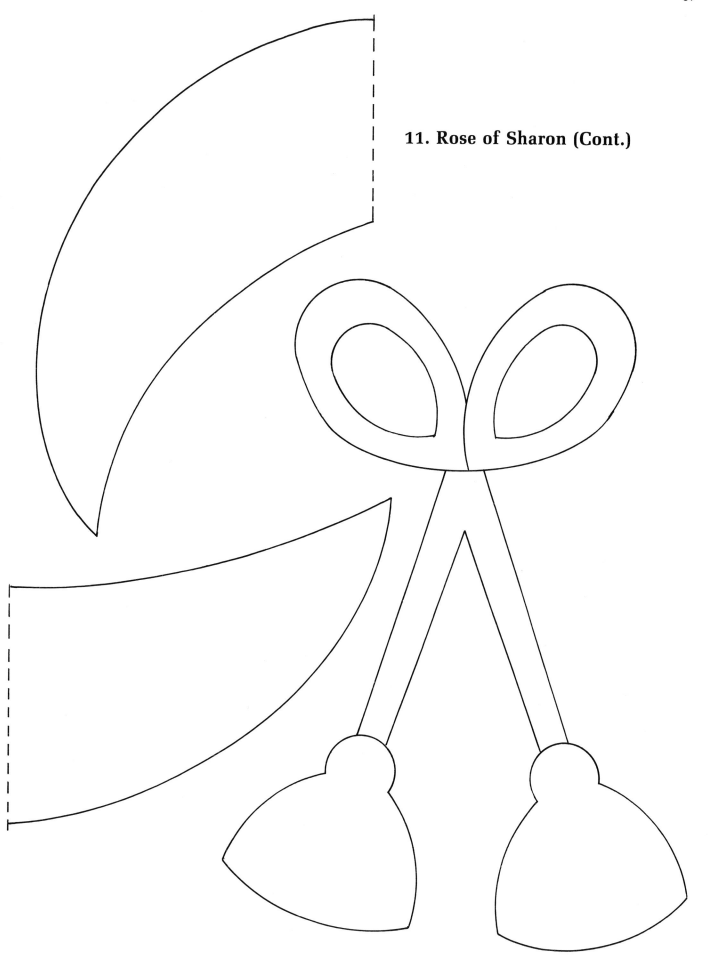

12. Washington Rose

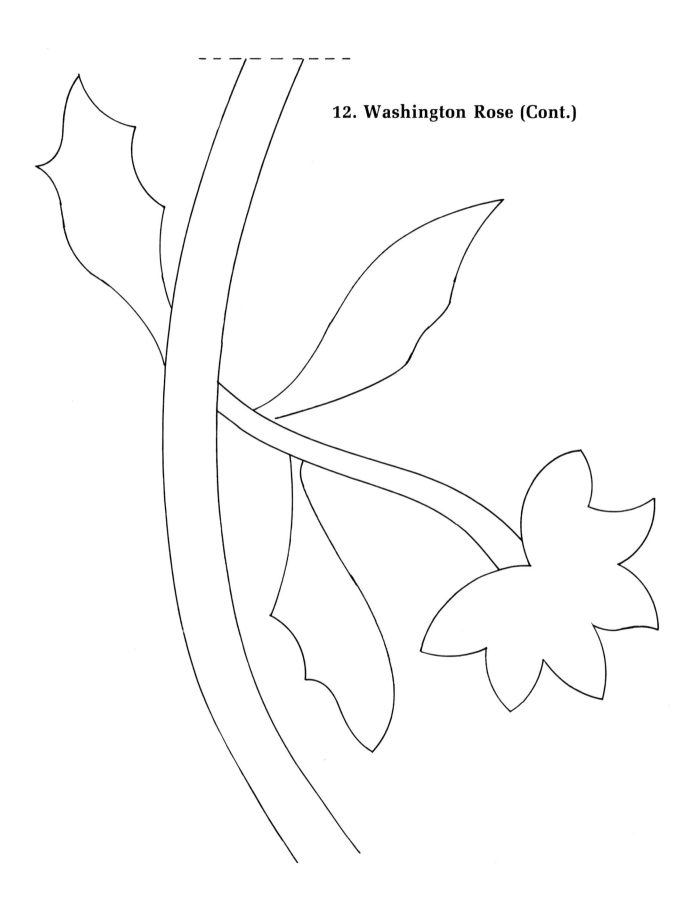

12. Washington Rose (Cont.)

12. Washington Rose (Cont.)

13. Four Tulips

14. Gwen's Tulip

15. Holland Queen

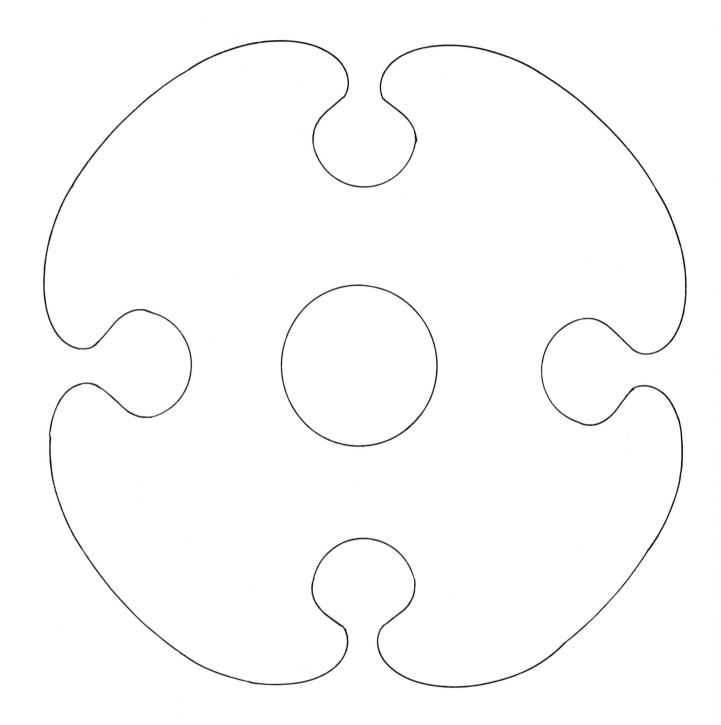

15. Holland Queen (Cont.)

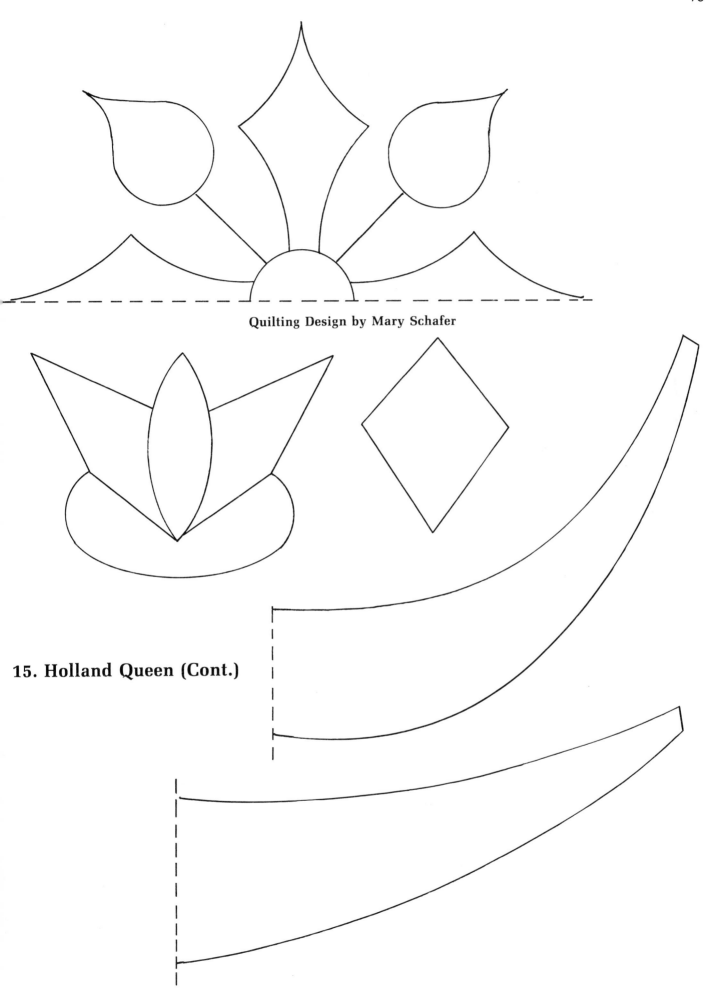

Quilting Design by Mary Schafer

15. Holland Queen (Cont.)

16. Minnie Roe's Tulip

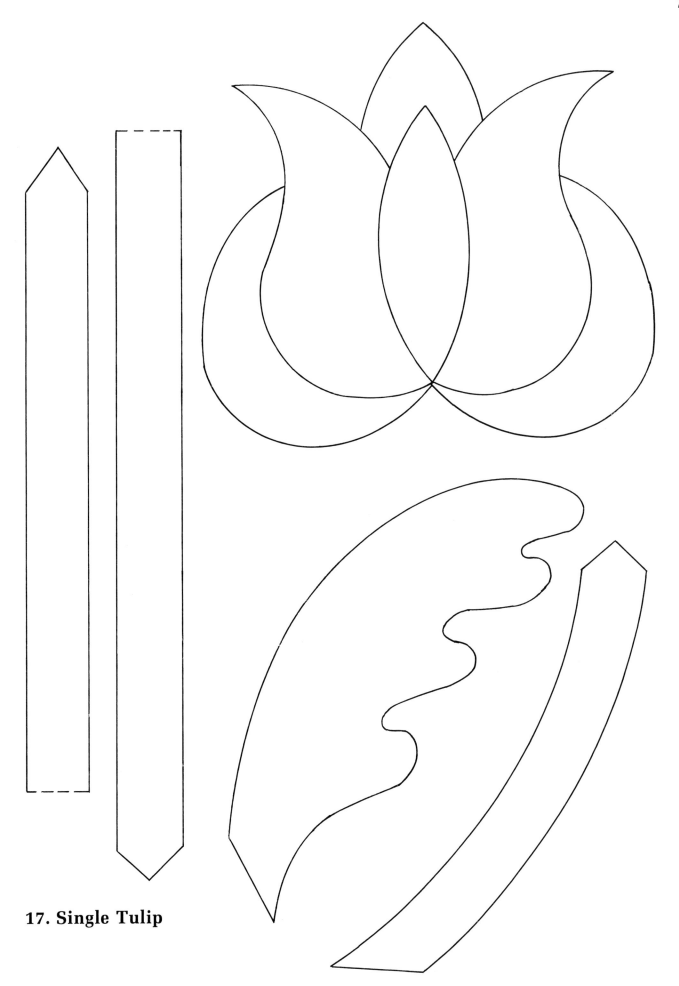

17. Single Tulip

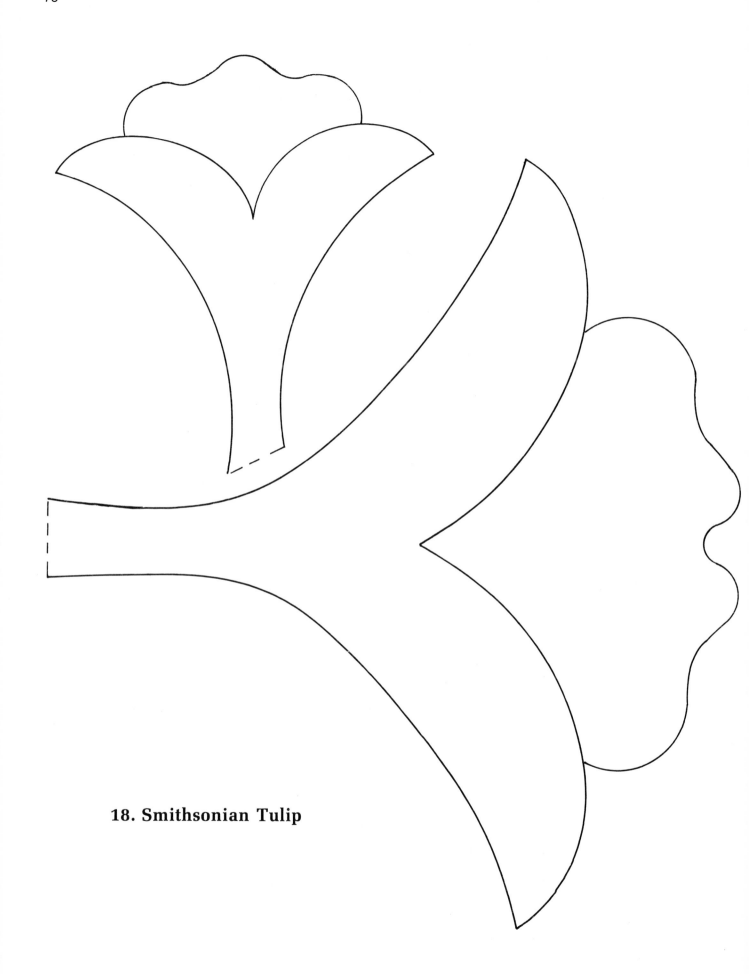

18. Smithsonian Tulip

18. Smithsonian Tulip (Cont.)

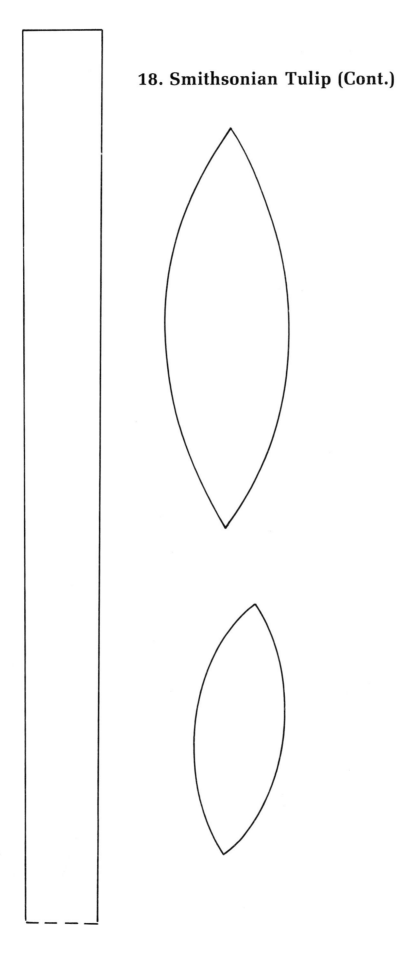

19. Tulip

20. Tulip

21. Tulip

21. Tulip (Cont.)

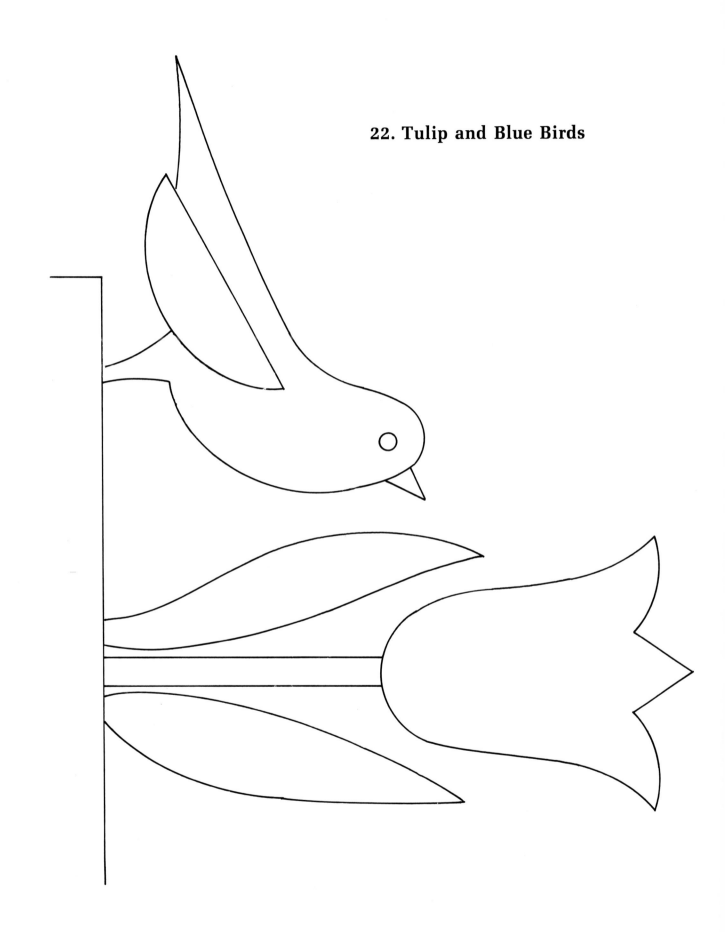

22. Tulip and Blue Birds

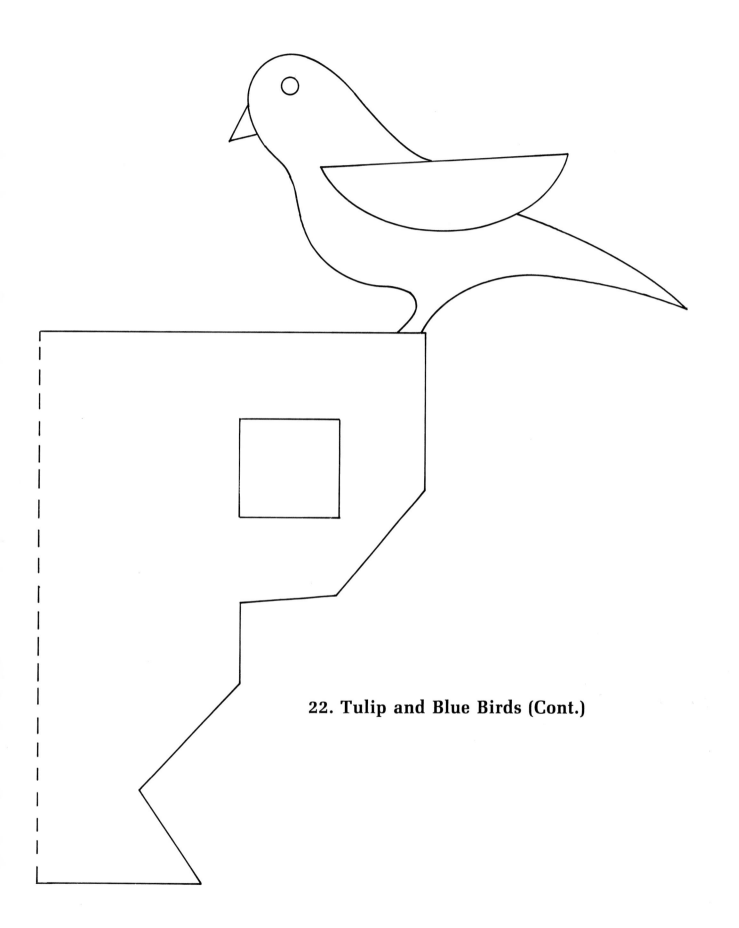

22. Tulip and Blue Birds (Cont.)

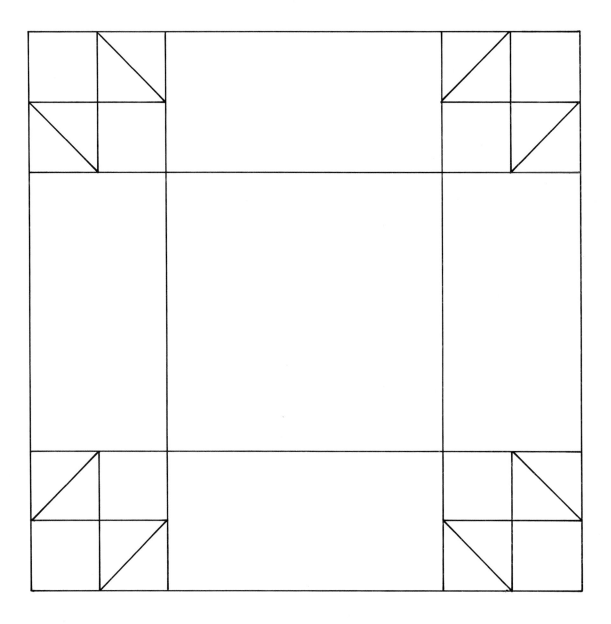

23. Tulip Lady Finger

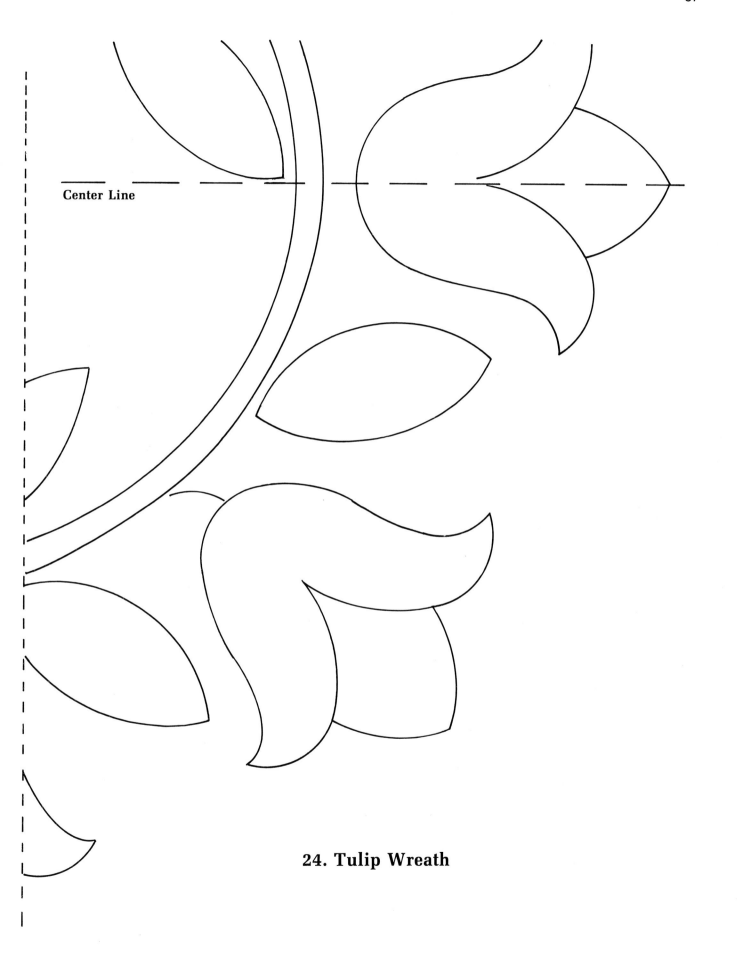

Center Line

24. Tulip Wreath

Appendix

"It is my feeling that applique quilts generally show less variety, invention and ingenuity than pieced quilts; the designs are often more static, colors more limited."

Jonathon Holstein, 1973

"I chose pieced designs rather than applique because the former are more easily indexed to design and there is less variation from maker to maker. A pieced LE-MOYNE STAR nearly always looks the same while no two COXCOMBS AND CURRANTS quilts seem to be from the same pattern source."

Barbara Brackman, 1983

"Applique offers free scope for one's fancy or artistic feeling, having no set design, no actual pattern that one must follow; therefore, no two appliqued quilts are ever exactly alike, either in detail or coloring."

Carrie Hall & Rose Kretsinger, 1935.

"Applique for quiltmaking came into favor about the middle of the 18th century and reached its climax about 1850. With the revival of patchwork in the 20th century it has reached a perfection of artistic color-combination and needlecraft far superior to anything made in earlier times."

Carrie Hall & Rose Kretsinger, 1935.

" . . . while the making of quilts has never been entirely discontinued, especially in some rural communities, and while present-day revaluation of the work of the old-time quiltmakers has encouraged a revival of the art, no well known pattern was evolved after 1880 . . . As a universal medium of feminine expression, quiltmaking ceased to exist. It vanished in the general night, as it were, of hideousness."

Ruth Finley, 1929

"The date 1880 definitely lets the curtain fall upon the old [world]. In the new, there would be no need for women to bend patient eyes and fingers over such tasks as patchwork."

Ruth Finley, 1929

"One of the popular methods for producing striking effects in applique resulted from the use of four great yard-square blocks . . . These four-block quilts, which went out of patchwork style before 1850, would be the joy of the modern decorator, but though many were made in their day they are now difficult to find. They saw harder usage than those of small designs, because, taking less time to make, they could be replaced more easily. Also the vogue for them did not last long, their patterns being too bold to suit the genteel fancies of the middle 19th century."

Ruth Finley, 1929

"To every mountain woman her piece quilts are her daily interest, but her patch (applique) quilts are her glory."

Miss Bessie Daingerfield,
Quoted by Marie Webster, 1915.

"Marriage quilts were often appliqued, and they usually required larger quantities of cloth of the same pattern than pieced quilts. Because appliqued versions were made as best quilts, they had a certain aura about them, and, although fewer were made, more have survived for the simple reason that they were seldom used."

Ruth McKendry, 1979

"A certain mystique dividing piece work and applique quilts has evolved in the literature on the subject, suggesting that piece work represents the meat and potatoes of quiltmaking and applique the dessert. We have found that, besides differences in technical execution, there is no other fundamental differentiation. Pieced quilts were not just used for 'everyday' wear, and applique quilts were not always put aside for the 'best' bed or for show or for the bride's trousseau."

Patsy and Myron Orlofsky, 1974

"Dutch women on Long Island and German girls in Pennsylvania took the stiff tulip from their painted chests and worked it into their unique patterns of wholly American patchwork.

American women changed the English Rose into the Cherokee Rose, the Prairie Wild Rose, and the Texas Rose that vies with the Lone Star . . ."

Rose Wilder Lane, 1963

"When one is talking today to women who did a great deal of quilting in their day, it is surprising how difficult it is to get them to give names to patterns, even common ones. They called their quilts some name or other when they were making it, but did not consider it as important as we do now . . . Pattern books were not common during the early days, the common patterns were known to most people, and they felt quite free to name their quilts as the fancy took them."

Ruth McKendry, 1979

"In the early days, the one aim and ambition of the Colonial woman seemed towards increasing the efficiency and happiness of life. Her stitches were lasting and executed with a loving hand, with disregard for length of time involved in the accomplishment. Today, although there seems to be a marked interest and revival of quilting, yet there is also a feeling of commercialization which tends towards lowering its sincerity and individuality as needle art. Women are depending more on the printed pattern sheet to save time and labor. These, having been used time and again, often become very tiresome."

Carrie Hall and Rose Kretsinger, 1935

The following article by Cuesta Benberry was first published in Nimble Needle Treasures *in March, 1974. We asked her permission to reprint it here for what it shows about the popularity of rose patterns.*

A Quilt Pattern Collector's Project State Rose Quilt Patterns

by Cuesta Benberry

Most quilt pattern collectors will agree, I'm sure, that it takes very little to get us started on a project. The project about which I'm reporting is not a recent project. We started it quite a few years ago. One day, just as quilt pattern collectors love to do, I was enjoying myself reading a group of Nancy Cabot quilt clippings. They read better than any novel. I picked up one – "Iowa Rose."

It stated, "Every state in the union has contributed to the quilt album with a rose pattern bearing its name."

Well, that did it! If, as the clipping stated, there are those quilt patterns for each state, why not try to find them? There were 48 states when the clipping was printed, so that meant looking for 48 patterns of state roses. Out came the pattern lists, the boxes of patterns, the books, the magazines, the scrapbooks, and the usual paraphenalia quilt pattern colletors use.

First, I'd see how many state rose quilt patterns I already had. After an hour or so of searching, I had mixed feelings about this proposed project. I had located some of the patterns, but at least a half-dozen or so were versions and variations of rose patterns for the same state – the Ohio Rose!

Now, I know that the quilt pattern collectors among you are way ahead of me. They know, without my saying, what the next step will be. They're right! I fired off letters to my quilt patterns collecting friends for help. From that beginning, we were off on a state rose quilt pattern safari. And no big game hunter's safari in the wilds of Africa was more fun than our state rose quilt pattern one here in the U.S. It was an enjoyable, though incomplete, project. We got for some states several versions or variations; for other states, we didn't find one. Ohio kept its lead in the number of variations with Kentucky as a close second.

Some patterns came from familiar sources, others came from unknown sources. We found more than the 48 we originally looked for but, of course, the number was inflated by the multiple versions we found. I think the crowning point of the project came when Ruth Snyder of Independence, Kansas, shared an old Ohio Rose version that had come from a radio station as a premium in the early days of radio broadcasting in the first quarter of the 1900's. A radio source is a rare source, if I've ever heard of one.

We got multiple versions of rose patterns from many states, including Texas, Indiana, Iowa, Pennsylvania, California, North Carolina, Missouri, New Jersey, Louisiana, North Dakota, Tennessee among others. For states, such as Alabama, Arkansas, Kansas, Delaware, Georgia, Illinois and Wisconsin we scraped by with a single version of a state rose quilt pattern. The states that eluded us completely, and we were unable to locate even one state rose quilt pattern for included New Hampshire, Montana and Minnesota.

Often, we'd find later versions of states having rose quilt patterns named for them. However, the original "Iowa Rose" Nancy Cabot clipping, that got us started on the project, was published in the 1930's. So we decided on an arbitrary cut-off date, not later than the publication date of the Nancy Cabot clipping. The pattern had to be of a quilt known to be in existence prior to this time. For our project could not be considered authentic if we included patterns of quilts known to have been made after Nancy Cabot reported they were already in existence. We were looking for quilts that had been made from the beginning of quiltmaking in the U.S. to the 1930's that had a state rose quilt design.

We were never able to determine which was the oldest state rose quilt pattern. We found several that were of early 1800's origin. We could not date any back to the late 1700's as we had hoped to do.

One little interesting fact we found was that in the really old versions (1800's origin), the name "Beauty" was sometimes, but not always, used interchangeably for state rose quilt patterns. An old version of the Ohio Rose was also called Ohio Beauty; an old Iowa Rose was called Iowa Beauty, too. Likewise for Missouri Beauty, among others. Two notable exceptions to this are New York Beauty and Alabama Beauty, which are not rose patterns at all. However, the synonymous names occured frequently enough so that if we located an old rose pattern named for a state with Beauty in the title, and from an obscure source, we would double check to see if this pattern also carried just the state name coupled with the word 'rose.'

Most of the state rose quilt patterns were applique designs, with a number of the 20th century ones being embroidery designs. There were a few pieced ones in the group.

As usual, we claim no originality for the idea of this project. For as any veteran quilt pattern collector knows, just mention any project, and there's always someone who has done it before you ever thought of it. Original project? I doubt it. Fun project? But definitely! And will someone please tell me what the Montana Rose quilt pattern looks like?

Reference Section

This reference section is a result of our method of making quilts. Whenever we start a new quilt, we pore over our books to look at similar quilts for ideas.

Because pattern names only became widely agreed upon and used during this century, and most of these quilts are from the last, we have listed them according to design type instead of pattern name. Therefore, you might look up a quilt that we refer to as a "Wreath" quilt, only to find another author calls it "President's Wreath," or, "Rose Wreath with Lotus." We were concerned with **design types**, not names.

Most of the books listed are in print and widely available, but there are a few listings from hard-to-find books, such as *Quilts in America*, which we use so often we felt we must include. This is not a complete listing of our sources, nor of all the examples in print, merely a list of some of our favorites. A complete list of our sources is given in the bibliography.

Here we used the author's last name for the listings. If the author has more than one book listed in our bibliography, we used an abbreviation of the title to which we refer. The *Quilt Engagement Calenders* published by E.P. Dutton are listed as "QEC, (date)." The annual *Quilt Digest* is listed as "QD, (date.)" If a quilt is shown in two books, we list both.

WHIG ROSE type: Complex center with four curved branches.
Bishop, New Discoveries, #113, #148.
Bishop, Secord, Weissman, p. 162.
Brackman, American Patchwork Quilt, #40, #49.
Bresenhan, Puentes, p. 57.
Florence, #42, #103.
Haders, plate 30.
Houck, Miller, p. 190.
Irwin, p. 10, p. 59.
Kentucky Quilts, plate 60.
Lipsett, p. 91.
McKendry, #308, #309, #314.
Nelson, Houck, #12.
Orlofsky, fig.s 65, 94.
Safford, Bishop, #234, #236.
Texas Quilts, pp. 25, 66.

Four Block Whig Roses
Fox, 19th Cent. APQ, #14.
Nelson, Houck, #161.
QD, 1987, p. 15.
QEC, 1975, #27.
Safford, Bishop, #270.

CENTER ROSE: Symmetrical center rose with leaves or buds, no stem.
Bishop, New Directions, #114.
Brackman, American Patchwork Quilt, #9.

Irwin, pp. 46, 54.
McClosky, p. 29.
Orlofsky, fig. 37.
Ramsey, Waldvogel, #5, #9.
Safford, Bishop. #244, #249.
Texas Quilts, pp. 100, 111.
Woodard, Greenstein, #84.

FLOWER ON STEM: Realistic rose or tulip on central stem, with leaves, buds, branches or secondary blossoms.
Roses
Bishop, New Discoveries, #147.
Bishop, Secord, Weissman, p. 170.
Bresenham, Puentes, p. 85.
Florence, #23, #25.
Haders, #30-7.
Havig, pp. 22, 23.
Irwin, p. 57.
Lasansky, Pieced by Mother, plates 53, 64.
McKendry, #302, #310, #315.
Michigan Quilts, #65.
QEC, 1988, #2.
Ramsey, Waldvogel, #41.
Safford, Bishop, #248, #288.
Texas Quilts, p. 102.

Tulips
Haders, #30-9.
Holstein, plate 64.
Houck, Miller, p. 51.
Lasansky, Heart of Penn., p. 36.
McKendry, #301, #312.
Orlofsky, fig. 177.
Safford, Bishop, #290.

WREATH DESIGNS: Wreath with leaves and flowers; roses, tulips or both.
Bishop, Secord, Weissman, p. 168.
Brackman, American Patchwork Quilt, #10, #11.
Florence, #31.
Fox, 19th Cent., #12, #13.
Fox, Small Endearments, fig. 22, plate 14.
Haders, #32-2, #32-5.
Havig, p. 20.
Irwin, p. 83.
Lasansky, Heart of Penn., p. 33.
Lasansky, Pieced by Mother, plates 58, 59.
McClosky, pp. 24, 25.
McKendry, #134, #135, #136, #313.
Michigan Quilts, #30, #44, #66.
Nelson, Houck, plate 2.
QEC, 1986, #27.
Safford, Bishop, #242, #243.
Texas Quilts, p. 48.
Woodard, Greenstein, #71, #80.

CROSSED STEM: Two or more stems with flower on each, either rose or tulip, sometimes with a design in the middle, extra leaves or branches.

Rose

Bishop, New Discoveries, #129.
Bishop, Secord, Weissman, p. 165.
Bresenhan, Puentes, p. 105.
Irwin, p. 60.
Kentucky Quilts, #38.
Michigan Quilts, #40, #145.
Nelson, Houck, #37.

Tulip

Brackman, American Patchwork Quilt, #8.
Florence, #153, #154.
Haders, #30-11, #30-12, #30-14, #30-15, #30-16.
Houck, Miller, pp. 103, 156.
Irwin, p. 71.
Lasansky, Pieced by Mother, plate 3.
McClosky, p. 27.
Michigan Quilts, #63, #64.
Nelson, Houck, plate 48.
Safford, Bishop, #293.
Texas Quilts, pp. 26, 65, 122.

ROSE TREE: A large "U" shape with fancy flowers, leaves, buds.
Brackman, American Patchwork Quilt, #47.
Bresenhan, Puentes, pp. 41, 49.
Haders, #32-3.
Irwin, p. 61.
Orlofsky, fig. 178.
Safford, Bishop, #241, #271.
The Denver Art Museum, #48.

Quilter's Choice, p. 38. (This is a Tulip Tree, rare, beautiful.)

FLOWER POT: An appliqued pot of fairly realistic flowers, roses or tulips or both.
Bishop, New Discoveries, #119.
Bresenhan, Puentes, p. 37.
Florence, #6, #45.
Haders, #31-3.
Michigan Quilts, #52.
Nelson, Houck, #74, #149, #181.
Orlofsky, fig. 71, plate 25.
QEC, 1981, #24.
QEC, 1988, #37.
QD, 1984, p. 52.
QD, 1987, p. 13.
Ramsey, Waldvogel, #43.
Safford, Bishop, #238, #240, #246, #273.
Woodard, Greenstein, #1, #76.

Four Block Flower Pots

Bishop, New Discoveries, #152.

Brackman, American Patchwork Quilt, #43.
Bresenhan, Puentes, p. 75.
Fox, 19th Cent., #5.
Haders, #31-4.
Lasansky, Heart of Penn., p. 38.
Nelson, Houck, #60, #173.
Orlovsky, plate 102.
QD, 1985, p. 49.
Safford, Bishop, #275, #279.
Texas Quilts, p. 22.

SINGLE TULIP: Inexplicably called "Single," this design type has three appliqued tulips on stems.
Florence, #27.
Havig, p. 16.
Houck, Miller, p. 67.
Michigan Quilts, #147, #158.
McKendry, #311.
Ramsey, Waldvogel, #2.
Texas Quilts, p. 134.

LONE STAR WITH ROSE OR TULIP EMBELLISHMENT
Florence, #81.
Haders, #17-6.
Michigan Quilts, #118, #119.
Nelson, Houck, #20.
Orlovsky, plate 13.
QD, 1983, p. 41.
QEC, 1982, #18.
Woodard, Greenstein, #22, #39.

OTHER QUILTS WHICH CONTAIN ROSES AND/OR TULIPS
Bishop, Secord, Weissman, p. 121.
Florence, #22.
Fox, 19th Cent., plates 15, 19.
McKendry, #262.
Orlovsky, fig. 198, plates 23, 30.
QD, 1985, p. 39.
QEC, 1979, #41, #47.
QEC, 1987, #15.
QEC, 1988, #53.
Texas Quilts, p. 38.
Woodard, Greenstein, #77.

RANDOM SAMPLERS
Haders, #41-10.
Lasansky, Pieced by Mother, plate 33.
Orlovsky, fig. 132.
QEC, 1975, #47.
QEC, 1980, #3.
Texas Quilts, p. 85.

SMALL QUILTS MADE FROM ONE LARGE ROSE OR TULIP BLOCK
Florence, #16.
Fox, Small Endearments, fig.s 23, 55, plates 37, 42.
Woodard, Greenstein, #79, #81.

Index

Quilts

1. BIRTHDAY ROSE 20
2. CROSS-STITCH ROSE 20
3. DEMOCRATIC ROSE 21
4. DEMOCRATIC ROSE 21
5. LEE'S ROSE AND BUDS 22
6. LEE'S ROSE AND BUDS 22
7. MISSOURI ROSE TREE 22
8. RADICAL ROSE 23
9. ROSES 23
10. ROSES AND HEARTS 24
11. ROSES AND HEARTS 24
12. ROSE AND TULIP WREATH 25
13. ROSE OF SHARON 26
14. ROSE OF SHARON 26
15. ROSE OF SHARON 26
16. ROSE WREATH 27
17. ROSE WREATH 27
18. WASHINGTON ROSE 28
19. WHIG ROSE 29
20. WHIG ROSE 29
21. WHIG ROSE 29
22. CLEVELAND TULIP 30
23. CROSSED TULIP 30
24. FULL BLOWN TULIP 31
25. GIANT TULIP 32
26. GWEN'S TULIP 32
27. HOLLAND QUEEN 33
28. LONE STAR AND TULIPS 33
29. MRS. EWER'S TULIP 34
30. PENNSYLVANIA DUTCH FLOWER GARDEN   34
31. SINGLE TULIP 35
32. SINGLE TULIP 35
33. SINGLE TULIP 35
34. SMITHSONIAN TULIP 36
35. TULIP 37
36. TULIP 37
37. TULIP 37
38. TULIP AND OAK LEAF 38
39. TULIP POT AND CHERRIES 38
40. TULIP SAMPLER 39
41. TULIP SAMPLER 40
42. TULIP TREE AND BUNNIES 40
43. UNCONVENTIONAL TULIP 41
44. EAGLE 41

Blocks

1. Martha Washington Rose 8
2. Mexican Rose 8
3. Michigan Rose 9

4. Old English Rose 9
5. Rose 10
6. Rose and Tulip 10
7. Rose Wreath 11
8. Rosebud 11
9. San Jose Rose 12
10. Wild Rose 12
11. Dutch Tulip 13
12. Full Blown Tulip 13
13. Lombardy Lady 14
14. Tulip 14
15. Tulip 15
16. Tulip 15
17. Tulip 16
18. Tulip and Bluebirds 16
19. Tulip in Vase 17
20. Tulip Lady Finger 17
21. Tulip Pot 18
22. Tulip Wheel 18

Other Applique Examples

1. Marie Webster Patterns 19
2. Tulip, Hand Towels 19
3. Windblown Tulip, Pillowslip 19

Patterns

1. Iowa Rose 46
2. Lee's Rose and Buds 47-48
3. Martha Washington Rose 49
4. Mexican Rose 50
5. Michigan Rose 51-52
6. Missouri Rose Tree 53-59
7. Old English Rose 60-62
8. Radical Rose 63
9. Rose Wreath 64
10. Rosebud 65
11. Rose of Sharon 66-67
12. Washington Rose 68-70
13. Four Tulips 71
14. Gwen's Tulip 72
15. Holland Queen 73-75
16. Minnie Roe's Tulip 76
17. Single Tulip 77
18. Smithsonian Tulip 78-79
19. Tulip 80
20. Tulip 81
21. Tulip 82-83
22. Tulip and Blue Birds 84-85
23. Tulip Lady Finger 86
24. Tulip Wreath 87

Bibliography

Alexander, Vera C. *Patchwork and Applique*. London: Sir Isaac Pitman and Sons, 1931.

Benberry, Cuesta, "Quilts in the Museum of History and Technology Smithsonian Institution, Washington, DC." *Nimble Needle Treasures*, (Summer, 1972.)

_____. "A quilt Pattern Collector's Project: State Rose Quilt Patterns." *Nimble Needle Treasures*. (March, 1974): 2-5.

_____. "Afro-American Women and Quilts." *Uncoverings 1980*. (1980) 64-67.

Bishop, Robert and Patricia Coblentz. *New Discoveries in American Quilts*. New York: E.P. Dutton and Company, Inc., 1975.

Bishop, Robert, William Secord and Judith Reiter Weissman. *Quilts, Coverlets, Rugs and Samplers*. New York: Alfred A. Knopf, 1982.

Bowne, Marty. "Friendship Bridges the Generation Gap." *American Quilter*. (Summer, 1987) 21-25.

_____. "American Quilter's Society Show and Contest Winners." *American Quilter*. (Fall, 1987) 19-47.

Brackman, Barbara. *American Patchwork Quilt: Quilts from the Spencer Museum*. Kokusai Art, Tokyo, Japan 1987.

_____. *An Encyclopedia of Pieced Quilt Patterns*. Lawrence, Kansas: Prairie Flower Publishing, 1979.

_____. "Dating Old Quilts Parts I-VI." *Quilter's Newsletter Magazine*, Issues 165-170.

_____. "A Chronological Index to Pieced Quilt Patterns 1775-1825." *Uncoverings 1983*. (1983) 99-127.

Bresenhan, Karoline and Nancy O'Bryant Puentes. *Lone Stars: A Legacy of Texas Quilts, 1836-1936*. Austin, Texas: University of Texas Press, 1986.

Carlisle, Lillian Baker. *Pieced Work and Applique Quilts at the Shelburne Museum*. Shelburne Museum pamphlet series #2. Shelburne, Vermont, 1957.

Cunningham, Joe. "An Old Fashioned Sampler." *Lady's Circle Patchwork Quilts*, March, 1986, 56-64.

_____. "Fan Quilting." *Lady's Circle Patchwork Quilts*, November, 1986, 50-54.

_____. "Fourteen Quilts Begun by One Woman and Finished by Another." *Uncoverings 1986*. (1986) 61-71.

Cunningham, Joe and Gwen Marston. "Applique." *Lady's Circle Patchwork Quilts*, January, 1988, 78-81.

Curtis, Phillip H. *American Quilts in the Newark Museum Collection*. Newark, NJ. The Newark Museum, 1974.

DeGraw, Imelda. *Quilts and Coverlet*. Denver, CO: Denver Art Museum, 1974.

Dewhurst, C. Kurt, Betty Mac Dowell and Marsha Macdowell. *Artists in Aprons*. New York: E.P. Dutton and Company, Inc., 1979.

_____. *Religious Folk Art in America*. New York: E.P. Dutton and Company, Inc., 1983.

Finley, John. *Kentucky Quilts 1800-1900*. New York: Pantheon Books, 1982.

Finley Ruth E. *Old Patchwork Quilts and the Women Who Made Them*. Philadelphia, PA: J.B. Lippincott, 1929.

Florence, Cathy Gains. *Collecting Quilts*. Paducah, KY: American Quilter's Society, 1985.

Fox, Sandi. *19th Century American Patchwork Quilt*. Tokyo, Japan: The Seibu Museum of Art, 1983.

_____. *Small Endearments: 19th Century Quilts for Children*. New York: Charles Scribner's Sons, 1985.

Frye, L. Thomas. *American Quilts: A Handmade Legacy*. Oakland, California: The Oakland Museum, 1981.

Haders, Phyllis. *The Warner Collector's Guide to American Quilts*. New York: Warner Books, Inc., 1981.

Hall, Carrie A. and Rose Kretsinger. *The Romance of the Patchwork Quilt in America*. Coldwell, Idaho: Caxton Printers Ltd., Bonanza Books, 1935.

Havig, Bettina. *Missouri Heritage Quilts*. Paducah, Kentucky: American Quilter's Society, 1986.

Hinson, Dolores A. *A Quilter's Companion*. New York: Arco Publishing, Inc., 1979.

Holstein, Jonathon. *The Pieced Quilt: An American Design Tradition*. Boston: New York Graphic Society, 1973.

Houck, Carter and Myron Miller. *American Quilts and How to Make Them*. New York: Charles Scribner's Sons, 1975.

Ickis, Marguerite. *The Standard Book of Quiltmaking and Collecting*. New York: Dover Publications, Inc., 1949.

Irwin, John Rice. *A People and Their Quilts*. Exton, Pennsylvania: Schiffer Publishing Ltd., 1983.

Kiracofe, Roderick. "Showcase." *The Quilt Digest*. (1983): 30-49.

_____. "Showcase." *The Quilt Digest*. (1985): 36-59.

Lane, Rose Wilder. *Woman's Day Book of American Needlework*. New York: Simon and Schuster, 1963.

Lasansky, Jeannette. *In the Heart of Pennsylvania: 19th and 20th Century Quiltmaking Traditions*. Lewisburg, Pennsylvania: Oral Traditions Project, 1985.

_____. *Pieced by Mother*. Lewisburg, Pennsylvania: Oral Traditions Project, 1987.

Lipsett, Linda Otto. *Remember Me: Women and Their Friendship Quilts*. San Francisco: The Quilt Digest Press, 1985.

Long, Patricia. "Pennsylvania Pillowslips." *The Quilter's Journal*. (Summer, 1979): 6, 10.

Marston, Gwen and Joe Cunningham. *Sets and Borders*. Paducah, Kentucky: American Quilter's Society, 1987.

Massey, Patricia. "Craft or Art? American Style Perplexes Japanese Visitors." *The Crafts Report*. (October, 1987): 15.

McCall's Heirloom Quilts. New York: The McCall Pattern Company, 1974.

McCall's How-to Quilt It. New York: The McCall Pattern Company, 1973.

McClosky, Marsha. *Christmas Quilts*. Bothell, Washington: That Patchwork Place, Inc., 1985.

McKendry, Ruth. *Quilts and Other Bedcoverings in the Canadian Tradition*. Toronto, Canada: Discovery Books, 1979.

McKim, Ruby. *101 Patchwork Patterns*. New York: Dover Publications, Inc. 1962.

Michigan Quilts. (Marsha MacDowell and Ruth Fitzgerald editors.) East Lansing, Michigan: Michigan State University Museum, 1987.

Montgomery, Florence M. *Textile in America: 1650-1870.*. New York: W.W. Norton & Company, Inc., 1984.

Mountain Mist Catalogue of Classic Quilt Patterns. Cincinnati, Ohio: The Stearns Technical Textiles Company, n.d.

Nelson, Cyril (ed.), *The Quilt Engagement Calender*. New York: E.P. Dutton and Company, Inc., 1975-1988.

Nelson, Cyril and Crter Houck. *Treasury of American Quilts*. New York; Crown Publishers, Inc., 1982.

Nesbitt, Margot L. *A Century of Quilts*. Oklahoma: Oklahoma Historical Society, n.d.

O'Dowd, Karen. "For Love Or Money." *Lady's Circle Patchwork Quilts*. (October/November, 1987): 16-36.

Orlovsky, Patsy and Myron. *Quilts in America*. New York: McGraw-Hill Book Company, 1974.

Paul, Velma Mackay. "Flower Album." *Country Gentleman*. October, 1941. (Reprinted in *The Quilters' Journal*, #30, Joyce Gross, ed., Mill Valley, California.)

Quilt Patterns: Patchwork an Applique. St. Louis, Missouri: Ladies Art Company, 1928. (Reprinted by Barbara Bannister, Alanson, Michigan, 1977.)

Quilts from Nebraska Collections. Lincoln, Nebraska: University of Nebraska, 1973.

Quilter's Choice: Quilts from the Museum Collection. Lawrence, Kansas: The University of Kansas, 1978.

Ramsey, Bets and Marikay Waldvogel. *The Quilts of Tennessee: Images of Domestic Life Prior to 1930*. Nashville, Tennessee: Rutledge Hill Press, 1986.

_____. "Roses Real and Imaginary: Nineteenth Century Botanical Quilts of the Mid-South." *Uncoverings 1986*. (1986) 9-25.

Safford, Carleton, L. and Robert Bishop. *America's Quilts and Coverlets*. New York: E.P. Dutton and Company, Inc., 1972.

Sexton, Carlie. *Old Fashioned Quilts*. 1928. (Reprinted by Barbara Bannister, Alanson, Michigan, 1964.

_____. *Yesterday's Quilts in Homes of Today*. 1930. (Reprinted by Barbara Bannister, Alanson, Michigan, 1964.)

Texas Heritage Quilt Society. *Texas Quilts: Texas Treasures*. Paducah, Kentucky: American Quilter's Society, 1986.

Todaro, Sandra M. "A Family of Texas Quilters and Their Work." *Uncoverings 1984*. (1984) 71-81.

Walker, Michele. *The Complete Book of Quiltmaking*. New York: Alfred A. Knopf, 1986.

Webster, Marie. *Quilts: Their Story and How to Make Them*. Detroit, Michigan: The Gale Research Company, 1972. Doubleday, Page and Company, 1915.

Woodard, Thomas K. and Blanche Greenstein. *Crib Quilts and Other Small Wonders*. New York: E.P. Dutton and Company, 1981.

Other Books by the Authors

Sets and Borders, AQS, 1987
Amish Quilting Patterns, Dover Publications, Inc., 1987
70 Classic Quilting Patterns, Dover, 1987
Q is for Quilt, MSU Museum, 1987

Other Books Published By AQS

Original Quilting Designs by Loraine Neff. . . . . $ 7.95

America's Pictorial Quilts by Caron Mosey $19.95

Award Winning Applique Technique by Carolyn and Wilma Johnson $17.95

Thimbles and Accessories, Antique and Collectible by Averil Mathis $19.95

Missouri Heritage Quilts by Bettina Havig $14.95

Quilt Art Annual Engagement Calendar by AQS . . . . $ 8.95

Texas Quilts, Texas Treasures by Texas Heritage Quilt Society $24.95

Somewhere In Between: Quilts and Quilters of Illinois by Rita Barrow Barber $14.95

Scarlet Ribbons, American Indian Technique For Today's Quilters by Helen Kelley $15.95

Dear Helen, Can You Tell Me? . . . all about quilting designs by Helen Squire $12.95

Sets & Borders by Gwen Marston & Joe Cunningham. $14.95

Irish Chain Quilts by Joyce B. Peaden $14.95

The Grand Finale, A Quilter's Guide to Finishing Projects by Linda Denner $14.95

Collecting Quilts: Investments in America's Heritage by Cathy Florence $19.95

Add $2.00 additional for postage & handling.